Diary of Dr. Rosetta Hall
1892-1894

Volume 4

Rosetta Sherwood Hall

Life in the Eastern Hemisphere

Diary of Dr. Rosetta Hall 1890 Volume 3
© 2016 by Esther Foundation
www.estherfoundationusa.org
1119 Old North Gate Road
Colorado Springs, Colorado
USA

All rights reserved. No portion of this book may be reproduced, stored in a retrieval system, or transmitted in any form or by any means—electronic, mechanical, photocopy, recording, scanning, or other—except for brief quotations in critical reviews or articles, without the prior written permission of the author.

Preface

Dr. Rosetta Sherwood Hall was born in 1865 in Liberty, New York, the daughter of a well-to-do Christian farming family. She obtained a teacher's certificate at the age of sixteen, and after teaching at local schools for a few years, was sent in 1890 to the remote far eastern land of Korea to devote her life to medicine and missionary work under the auspices of the Woman's Medical Missionary Society of the Methodist Episcopal Church. She would go on to serve as a medical missionary there for forty-three years.

For hundreds of years, Korea had observed the 내외법 *Nae Wae Beop*, a Confucian law stipulating the strict segregation of gender. This law had restricted women's access to formal education, professional training, political representation, and movement in the public sphere. Missionaries like Dr. Rosetta Hall dedicated themselves not only to serving women who did not have access to proper medical care, but also to widely expanding these women's social opportunities and renewing their sense of self-esteem. With the heart of Christ, Dr. Rosetta Hall exercised love and compassion on Korea's underprivileged. Her significant achievements include adapting Braille into Korean script, which inaugurated a formalized education system for Korea's blind and deaf. She trained many girls and young women in the medical profession, giving them the knowledge and agency to care for their own people.

At the time of appointment, she was supposed to have served a five-year term in the field as a single missionary. Two years into her term, she married Rev. William James Hall, M.D., whom she met in the slums of New York City while they were working as medical missionaries there. Until Rev. Hall's tragic death by typhus fever in November 1894, they worked in Seoul, started work in Pyongyang, and began raising a newborn son, Sherwood.

After burying her beloved husband, Rosetta returned to New York with her infant son and a daughter in her womb. While in the States, she furthered the work she undertook in Korea. She oversaw the education of Esther Pak Kim, Korea's first female doctor of medicine, who received her M.D. degree in 1900 at the Baltimore Woman's Medical College; she raised funds and established the Hall Memorial Hospital in Pyongyang in February 1897; and she published a biography of her late husband in August 1897. It was during this time that Rosetta visited the New York Institute for the Blind and drew from New York Point to begin development of Korean Braille.[1]

She returned to Korea in 1897 with her two children to serve in Pyongyang, where she had begun pioneering mission work with her husband and had endured severe per-

---

[1] The first embossed book for the blind of Korea, the syllabary and first six lessons from Mrs. George Heber Jones' 초학언문 *Chyo Hók Eun-Mun* (*A Korean Primer* - nine cards, about 5½ x 9 inches, pricked on oiled Korean mulberry paper by hand in 1897), was donated to Taegu University School of Special Education by her granddaughter Phyllis Hall King in 1996 and is currently on display at the Rosetta Hall Museum Room.

secution. Shortly after her arrival, however, her 3-year-old daughter, Edith Margaret, died of dysentery. Rosetta suffered greatly from this loss, even more so than when she had lost her husband. She wrote in her diary a letter to her dead daughter:

> "Mamma can't help longing for a happier experience, and she has tried to lay her Isaac on the altar, and to let God do with her the best he can; and even where she may not have succeeded in this, it seems as if God himself has taken her most precious things, and she has tried to learn the lessons He would have her, and not be rebellious."

Rosetta's faith is remarkable in the face of her great personal losses. Despite her lack of understanding over their meaning, she said she "must just give her feelings over to Jesus and trust him implicitly."

In the summer of 1901, Dr. Rosetta Hall returned to New York for the second time, physically and mentally exhausted. After recuperating at the Castile Sanatorium for eight months, she again returned to Korea in the spring of 1903. Until her retirement in 1933, she remained steadfast in her work. She founded the Women's Medical Training Classes in Pyongyang and Seoul; her class in Seoul would later become the Women's Medical Institute, the precursor to Korea University's College of Medicine. She established four hospitals: the Baldwin Dispensary in Seoul (1892), the Woman's Hospital of Extended Grace in Pyongyang (1894), the Hall Memorial Hospital in Pyongyang (1897), and the

Chemulpo Woman's Hospital (1921). She also helped to establish the Edith Margaret Children's Wards in Pyongyang and the Child's Welfare Clinic in Seoul. Her work on behalf of the blind and deaf gained recognition throughout East Asia, leading to the Convention on the Education of the Blind and Deaf of the Far East, first held in Pyongyang in August 1914. Her forty-three years of service in Korea were a true testament to her resilience, her bravery, and her spirit. But they also testify to her religious conviction and purpose. In spite of the sacrifices she made and the losses she sustained, her obedience was drawn from the wellspring of her love for God and for the Korean people. God's provision, enacted through Dr. Rosetta Hall and many other devoted workers, liberated Korea's underprivileged—the women, the poor, and the handicapped—and privileged them anew as children of the King.

It is a blessing and an amazing grace that the work of transcribing and translating Dr. Rosetta Hall's diaries fell upon me. A faithful life is most precious in His eyes, and such a life is now able to be recorded, recognized, and passed down through the generations. I thank the Hall family for preserving and donating these diaries. The *Journal of Sherwood Hall*, in particular, passed through many hands in order to survive. Prior to his forced evacuation from Korea by the Japanese, Dr. Sherwood Hall had sent the journal to Miss Lund, who boarded the last evacuation boat to North America, the *S.S. Mariposa*. She brought it with her across the Pacific, and upon her arrival in Los Angeles, she sent it through post to Pastor Scott of Liberty, New York, to whom it arrived safely in December 1940.

After Dr. Rosetta Hall's death in 1951, two generations of the Hall family—her son Dr. Sherwood Hall, his wife Dr. Marian Hall, their daughter Mrs. Phyllis Hall King, and her husband Dr. Edward King, Jr.—have preserved these diaries over the course of sixty-four years. On January 1, 2015, Dr. and Mrs. King generously decided to offer the documents to the public.

I spent three days and nights with them in their home in McLean, Virginia, brainstorming about how to best benefit the public with the history, stories, and lessons written in the diaries. I was asked to translate the diaries into Korean and publish them in both Korean and English. In April 2015, all six diaries of Dr. Rosetta Hall (four diaries from 1890 – 1894 and two scrapbooks chronicling Sherwood and Edith's childhoods) were donated to the Yanghwajin Foreign Missionary Cemetery in Seoul, where Dr. Rosetta Hall and her five other family members are buried. The first diary of 1890 was published with a Korean translation in September 2015 as a highlight for Yanghwajin's Special Exhibition commemorating Dr. Rosetta Hall's 150th birthday. The rest of the volumes will be published over the next year.

Readers of both English and Korean will benefit from these volumes. Essentially, they were her scrapbooks. Many letters, photographs, newspaper articles, sketches, and notes, as well as locks of hair, clothing, and pressed flowers and leaves, are preserved in the books as primary sources. She had continued to add notes and memo clips to her original material as the years passed by, writing around the edges and filling in the open margins. I have left her materials and texts mostly in their original state, correcting only a few spelling errors and re-arranging some of the entries to reflect their chronology.

Since her girlhood days on a farm in Liberty, New York, Dr. Rosetta Hall loved God and strained to hear His voice. In spite of doubt and tribulation, she followed Him and obeyed His commands. She went to the land where no one else would go, and she fulfilled the good work that no one else would fulfill. She loved the people no one else seemed to love. She grew from the roots of God's Love and was able to stand up again and again throughout all her storms, in order to convey that Love to others. What a great mind, and a beautiful life!

I hope for the readers of these diaries to be blessed and inspired by Dr. Rosetta Hall's example.

Sue Kim
Colorado Springs
December 4, 2015

Letter from Rev. William James Hall, M.D.[2]

---

[2] Likely written in January 1892 as Rosetta and William James Hall decided to get married and were writing letters to their parents at home for approval. Rosetta's mother replied, "Yours of January 16 received." (see April 26, 1892 diary)

Diary of Dr. Rosetta Hall 1892-1894

My dear Rosetta,

How are you this evening? Mr. Jones is out and I am trying to discharge some of my neglected duties, i.e. writing letters. Will you please help me with one? You know your people much better than I do and I think you will be able to give me some helpful suggestions. I enclose one I thought of copying and sending to your father and mother. Please return it with any suggestions you may care to give.

Well Rosetta, I can't tell you how my heart goes out for you these days.

Already we are one in heart.

Our absence from each other has been like the tree in winter that is gathering up nourishment and preparing to bud and our meeting again like the effects of the balmy spring upon that tree causing it to give forth the blossoms which beautify, distributing their sweet odors to the surrounding atmosphere.

And I am sure this is only a foretaste of what God has in store for us. We will walk in the sunlight of His presence. Heaven begins here.

With much love,

Will

Diary of Dr. Rosetta Hall 1892-1894

Dr. William James Hall's List of Correspondences in January 1892

"Arta Bates, answered; Mrs. Dmitrievky, answered; Dr. Sherwood, answered; Omar L. Kilborn, answered (c/o Presbyterian Mission, Shanghai); Miss Rothweiler, answered (about R. S.); Miss Adams, answered; McArthur, answered; Copy of letter to Mr. Sherwood."

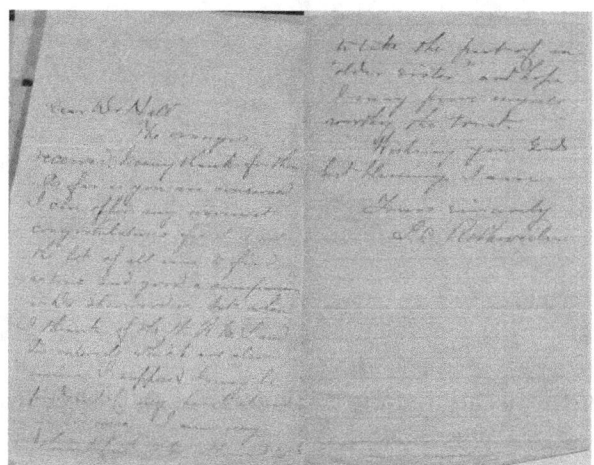

Undated[3] letter from Miss Rothweiler

---

[3] Likely written when Rosetta announced her decision to marry William James Hall.

Diary of Dr. Rosetta Hall 1892-1894

Dear Dr. Hall,

The oranges received. Many thanks for them. As far as you are concerned, I can offer my warmest congratulations for it is not the lot of all man to find as true and good a companion as Dr. Sherwood is but when I think of the W. F. M. S.[4] and its interests, which are also mine, I suppose I may be pardoned if my heart almost failed me. I am very thankful to be allowed to take the part of an "older sister" and hope I may prove myself worthy the trust.

Wishing you God's best blessings, I am
Yours sincerely,
L. C. Rothweiler

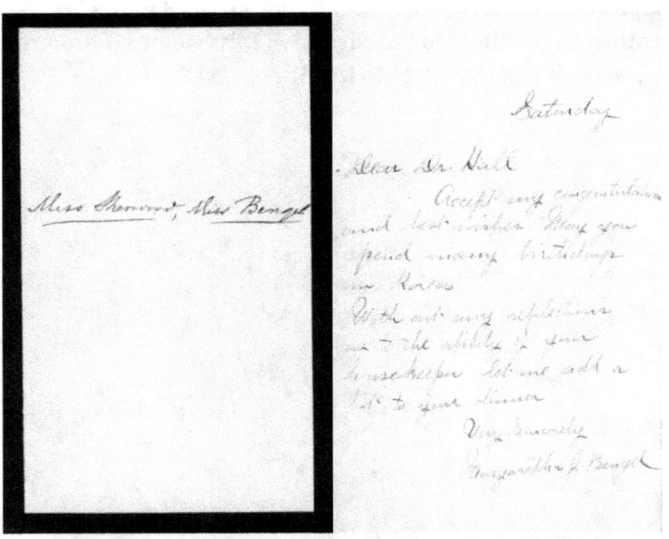

Birthday card to Rev. William James Hall, M.D. from "Miss Sherwood and Miss Bengel"[5]

---

[4] Woman's Foreign Missionary Society.
[5] William James Hall was born on January 16, 1860 and was housekeeping with Rev. George Heber Jones at this time.

Diary of Dr. Rosetta Hall 1892-1894

Saturday, January 16, 1892

Dear Dr. Hall,

Accept my congratulations and best wishes. May you spend many birthdays in Korea. Without any reflections as to the ability of your housekeeper let me add a bit to your dinner.

Very Sincerely,

Margaretha J. Bengel

Tuesday, March 8, 1892

Great peace have they which love thy law and nothing shall offend them. Ps. 119:165

> The loftiest test of friendship, understood as companionship, is the power to do without it. And in this world of external confusions and separations, there is often such need. ++ We turn our faces from each other, but never our hearts, and walk our opposite ways. ++ There is no danger of losing love here or hereafter if it is only real; for love is the one indestructible element in the universe.
> —Lucy Larcom

One week ago tonight, I bade my dear Doctor "goodbye," and the next day he started for a two months trip into the country in company with Rev. Jones. They expect to walk to "We Chu" up on the northwest boundary of Korea 350 miles. Our mission has some work up there that needs looking after, and both there and upon their way up they

Diary of Dr. Rosetta Hall 1892-1894

expect to do more or less evangelistic and medical work. May the Holy Spirit prepare much "good ground, such as hear the Word and receive it, and bring forth fruit some thirty-fold, some sixty, and some one hundred." Mark iv. 20.

It has been a busy week, and has passed by quickly, almost before I realize it here it is Tuesday night again. Since the New Year, Tuesday has been the evening of the week that we chose to spend together, so tonight I thought I would do use at least that much time every week to write in my journal, which I have not kept now since the last day of the Old Year.

We had a snowfall of some five inches Sunday, it is melting now. The roads were just beginning to dry up a little before, but now they are worse than ever. Many patients cannot come to the Dispensary, on account of the bad walking, yet more managed to get out than I'd expect. There were eight who came last Sunday upon purpose for the Sunday afternoon service in the Dispensary waiting room, and we had a good time. The old white-haired lady and her daughter-in-law (see December 6, 1891)[6] are still faithful attendants. They also come to Sunday school every morning, and often bring a friend with them. The old lady's husband came and we introduced him to Mr. Appenzeller, and he attends the men's meetings nearly every Sunday though he is quite a feeble old man. They seem to be really a converted family, with but little personal instruction they seem to have entered the Kingdom like little children. We

---

[6] For the story about this family, see Rosetta's December 6, 1891 diary and mission letter written on December 12, 1892 (Appendix 1).

Diary of Dr. Rosetta Hall 1892-1894

learned that before the Korean New Year, the old mother took down the 신주 *shinju* (ancestral tablets) before which they used to offer sacrifice. Her husband split them up, and the daughter-in-law put them in the fire. The latter is a widow, but told Miss Rothweiler without her ever having spoken to her upon the subject, that she would make no more offerings for the dead. Miss Rothweiler says, "But your son will," she said, "No his grandfather had commanded him not to." The son does not yet believe. He says it is all right for the old people as they will soon die, but he thinks he has plenty of time to consider it before he wants to go to heaven. One day when I asked different ones to pray at the close of our service, his mother prayed for this young man. In her prayer the old grandmother said, "Hitherto I have served the devil, but from henceforth, I desire to serve the Lord." They are such pleasant honest looking people, that one cannot help but to like their looks. Their actions do not belie. I have been asking Miss Rothweiler to speak to them about baptism, and to ask them to stay here Sunday night and part of Monday now and then, for further instruction. So far we have rather neglected them it seems to me.

I wonder where Dr. Hall is now. Have not heard from him since he left. Don't know whether I will or not. The traveling has been so bad, think they could scarcely have gotten to "Pyong Yang" yet. I miss him, but I am not impatient. I love him too much for that I think —so much, that I can be happy, very happy, even in his absence.

Diary of Dr. Rosetta Hall 1892-1894

Oh, I do thank God for my love. It has made me grow so much in many ways. And I believe it is indeed as Lowell says:

> "A love that shall be new and fresh each   hour
> As is the golden mystery of sunset
> Or the sweet coming of the evening star
> Alike, and yet most unlike, every day,
> And seeming ever best and fairest now."

Tuesday, March 22, 1892

I will mention the loving kindness of the Lord. Isa. lxiii. 7

> My heart was hot and restless
>   And my life was full of care
> And the burden laid upon me
>   Seemed greater than I could bear,
> But now it has fallen from me
>   It is buried in the sea
> And only the sorrow of others
>   Throws a shadow over me.
> —Longfellow

Last week I didn't have a time to write in my journal, and now there is so much to write that I don't believe I can crowd it into one evening.

Last Thursday I was very pleasantly surprised by receiving a letter from Dr. Hall dated 흥슈원[7]March 11th. He is

---

[7] Heungsuwon, a town located in the North Hwanghae Province.

Diary of Dr. Rosetta Hall 1892-1894

well and happy and feels that the trip will prove a blessing in every way. He had then treated to 60 patients, receiving for medicine for them 10250 cash, and 4975 cash for 78 books sold them. Many had been interested and several manifested a desire to become Christians.

It has kept us so cold, and we are still having snow quite often here in Seoul, so I fear it is not very pleasant traveling towards the North, and they are walking the most of the way. Mr. Han[8] the Korean evangelist that went with them says Dr. Hall would make a good general; he is such a walker.

The walking keeps so bad that the attendance at the dispensary has not increased much yet, and my outcalls still keep up. I have not been very well for a week now, though I've not given up to it yet. My old enemy " follicular tonsillitis " is hugging me tighter and tighter every day until both tonsils are so large they nearly meet and tonsils and arches are spotted all over with little ulcers from broken down follicles. I have such a pain, or rather dull ache that increases to pain when I cough, in the mastoid cells behind my right ear. So far have not had much fever—101°. I am in hopes the worst is passed now, and I will not have to lay by for it.

After I came up from the dispensary this afternoon, to my surprise, a good fat mail came. We were not expecting it until Friday. I received letters from Mother[9], Annie[10],

---

[8] Rev. Suk Jin Han. He was one of the first seven graduates of Pyong Yang Theological Seminary in 1907.
[9] Mrs. Rosevelt R. Sherwood (maiden name Phoebe Gildersleeve).

Diary of Dr. Rosetta Hall 1892-1894

Emma[11], Tempie[12], Rev. Scott[13], and Dr. Payne of Board of Education (sending back 2 of my notes given when in College. This makes 4 I have redeemed now), also a letter from Mrs. Skidmore[14] in reply to the one I wrote her December 29th. Dear Mrs. Skidmore! She is quite disgusted with me. She says, "As to my personal disappointment that is of little weight to you or anyone, even to myself in comparison with the disastrous effect of the loss of confidence in the Home workers who send the ladies abroad for special work." She reminds me that the W. F. M. S. contract requires five years service as a single woman, or the return of passage and outfit money.[15] This of course is all right and will be paid over gladly to send a new doctor out. I do hope Mrs. Skidmore may look at it a little differently in time. I think where she has misunderstood me the most has been in only thinking of what I felt and said at the time I sent my testimonials in and up to the time that I bade her goodbye before going home for the summer. I did feel then that I would not marry before five years, if at all. Yes, of course, I did, or I should never have sent my application in at all. And later after Dr. Hall visited me in my home and I wrote to Mrs. Skidmore and told her of what little hope I'd seen fit to give him. I was yet quite as strong in not want-

---

[10] Annie Sherwood, Rosetta's younger sister.
[11] Mrs. Emma C. Tice Sherwood is Rosetta's brother Dr. William Fanton Sherwood's wife.
[12] Temperance (Tempie) Gray is Rosetta's childhood friend.
[13] Rev. S. H. Scott of Rosetta's home church in Liberty, New York.
[14] Mrs. H. B. Skidmore was the corresponding secretary of the Woman's Foreign Missionary Society.
[15] See Rosetta's letter to the Methodist Mission written on April 12,1893 (Appendix 4).

Diary of Dr. Rosetta Hall 1892-1894

ing to marry before the five years had passed. I don't see why people should have any less confidence in my sense of duty, of my being able to tell what the Lord would have me do now, than before. Mrs. Skidmore then thought I was capable of knowing my duty in the matter, but now she questions it. But never mind, I am convinced it has all been for the best, and though it might look to some that I must have been mistaken in my sense of duty either when I came alone to Korea, or now, I believe I was not either time, and in God's own time perhaps it may look clearer to others, if not, I am not going to fret about it. It is my nature to want to please everybody, but where this clashes with pleasing God, I pray ever for strength to yield the former every time.

"Quotation from a letter of Mrs. Cowen to Miss Bengel"

"If you had gone out as Dr. S. did with the fixed intention of breaking your promise, I should feel glad you had left us, but as you really thought God wanted you and went out intending to make it your life work, I cannot feel you have wronged the work as Mrs. Skidmore does of Dr. S."

Diary of Dr. Rosetta Hall 1892-1894

At home they had not received my letter telling that we hoped to be married in June, but only the letter written December 17 merely stating that Dr. Hall had just arrived. They had not known of his coming for sure before, but from what they say they take it for granted now, that we will be married too soon. I can scarcely tell whether they are pleased or not, but would gather that Father and Annie are while probably mother and Joe are not. I shall be anxious to get answer from them to my next letter. Dr. Hall wrote also at the same time to Father and Mother.

Mother wrote of the death of my Aunt Emily[16] and Uncle Sam Bradley of Baltimore. They were both buried in one grave. Aunt Emily was Father's youngest sister. Father and Uncle Bradley Sherwood[17] are all that are left now.

Tempie writes me of the death of her "darling mother." It saddens her so much.

Oh, I do pray that our family may be spared to all meet at home once again. I am so thankful we have been kept thus far. Mother writes they are all well and Father is reading as usual. Rev. Scott wrote he never saw Father looking better.

Some pretty good news that the Scrantons will probably leave America April 5th and be with us early in May. That makes me very glad, and I think everybody, both for-

---

[16] Aunt Emily Sherwood (b. 1808) married Samuel Bradley around 1834.
[17] Uncle Bradley Burr Sherwood (b. 1813) was the youngest brother of Rosetta's father Rosevelt R. Sherwood.

Diary of Dr. Rosetta Hall 1892-1894

eigners and natives, will also be. Mrs. M. F. Scranton, especially, is very dear to the hearts of all.

Tuesday, March 29, 1892

Thus shalt thou say unto the children of Israel, <u>I am</u> hath sent me unto you. Ex. 3:14

> Do let us take time from the gathering, the talking, the doing, for the being. One of the most wonderful and blessed names of God is "<u>I am</u>."
> —Mrs. J. H. Knowles

> Small souls help by what they do, great souls by what they are.
> —Emerson

I spent the morning quite undisturbed in study. Am getting pretty well along in Part II of Underwood's grammars[18]. The rest of the day has been a complete holiday for me. I accepted an invitation to tiffin from Mrs. Appenzeller. It was a "dove party"[19] as Miss Bengel called it, of fourteen ladies, to celebrate the Land Anniversary of the "Ladies' Tennis Club." I surprised the folks by going. Miss Rothweiler remarked, "You'd not catch the doctor going to any such place last year if she could get rid of it." Well, I am be-

---

[18] *An Introduction to the Korean Spoken Language* by Horace Underwood. It is comprised of two parts, Part I focusing on the Korean grammar and Part II comparing the English and Korean grammars, with examples.
[19] Likely a borrowed expression from the U.S. political "hawks" and "doves."

Diary of Dr. Rosetta Hall 1892-1894

ginning to learn, perhaps a little late in life, that man is meant to be a sociable animal. I've always known it in a general way, but have ever felt quite willing to shirk my duty when it came to me in particular. However, I am able to do differently this year with a better conscience, than last year. I did not work so faithfully for nothing, but so trained my helpers that I can now often leave the work in their hands and feel confident it will not be neglected.

Here it is Tuesday night again, four weeks since the doctor has been gone. In one way I can scarcely realize it, and the time seems short; but in another, it seems long, and I am wanting to see him again, at least I wish I could hear from him. Neither Miss Bengel nor I have had any word since I last wrote in my journal. I think that is one reason why the time seems so long tonight.

Again we have had snow, and it still freezes nights. Always before, Miss Rothweiler says, we have had the garden planted by this time, but it can't be done this year.

Diary of Dr. Rosetta Hall 1892-1894

The "Dove Party."
Rosetta standing on the back row second from the left.

Dispensary patients are not many yet. Had a very bad case yesterday that I took into the hospital. It had been a very large carbuncle that nothing had been done for until it had dissected up the scalp from ear-to-ear half way to the crown of the head, and half of this was dead, and this dead skin and hair macerating with the pus and slough made the most foul odor I ever smelled. We smelled it from the waiting room before she came into the consulting room, and I thought it must be a bad uterine cancer or something of that sort. When she came in my girls shut the drug-room door and held their nose with their aprons. I cut away the dead parts and put them in the stove then irrigated with a 4 quarts of hot water strongly carbolized, dressed with Iodoform gauze, cotton and bandage, and the odor quite disappeared. I don't know whether she can recover or not;

Diary of Dr. Rosetta Hall 1892-1894

she has had it so long that I fear she has become poisoned by it. Her eyelids and face are edematous, but I will do what I can for her. She must certainly feel more comfortable.

During the week, I've been called several times to see a Chinese woman, the wife of the original "Steward," who started the foreign hotel and store in Chemulpo and Seoul. She has attacks of asthma. I've not found her so very badly off any time, but she felt that I helped her, and I've an idea [she] liked to see me too, and so she sent some times when it didn't seem to me necessary, and the last time she sent, it was on Sunday. I didn't go, but sent her a palliative with the messenger, who said himself she was no worse. I have not heard from her since.[20]

I have not been well myself. The most of the week, have felt miserable, have not slept well on account of coughing, but last night I slept quite well, and today have been better. Still feel some trouble in the mastoid region, and a few cervical glands are swollen upon that side. I am in hopes it is only sympathetical with the enlargement of that tonsil, and will disappear again but my throat is well. Esther wrote me this letter the other day.

> "I am sorry that you are not quite well. I hoped you would be quite well since your Dr. Hall went away but now you are sick and I am very very sorry. I cannot help you get better but our Heavenly Father will. I trust the Lord will make you well and strong. I do not know how to take care of sick people and I

---

[20] Rosetta added, "Later heard she was better."

Diary of Dr. Rosetta Hall 1892-1894

do not know what medicine they need. I am so sorry that your faithful doctor not here. If he stay his house then he comfort you and tell you what medicine you eat, and he will take care of you very well. By and by I will learn how take care of sick persons and learn how comfort them, then I will comfort as much as Dr. Hall comfort you. I must to close because it is time to study arithmetic."

Dear Esther, she is indeed my "truly comforter" as she sometimes signs herself. Her love and sympathy are a great help to me, and I thank the Lord for her.

> That love for one, from which there doth not spring
> Wide love for all, is but a worthless thing.
> —Lowell

Tuesday, April 5, 1892, 한식[21]

Trust in Him at all times; ye people, pour out your heart before him. God is a refuge for us. Selah (stop and think). Psa. lxii. 8

> "God knows. Oh, yes! What comfort 'tis
>   To know the eye that never sleeps
> Sees all that is, and every life
>   In ever watchful memory keeps.
> He knows just why that good must go,
>   He knows just why this ill must to stay
> We cannot know. We only "trust,"
>   Remembering that God knows the way."[22]

---

[21] 한식 *hanshik* (Cold Food Festival) is 105th day from the winter solstice, a day designated to eat cold food and to visit ancestral graves.

Diary of Dr. Rosetta Hall 1892-1894

Tuesday evening has come again and still there is no news from our wanderers; don't quite know what to make of it, but trust that all is well.

I have had another pretty good week, for me, at studying Korean. The first two days of the month were rainy, and there were but few patients, so that with Esther's help I got the Records all worked out for the last month. Also got along with my hospital accounts and financial report rather easier than usual, so I began the month quite square. I am housekeeper again this month, that I always dread beforehand and try my best to get out of, but don't mind it so much when I once get into it. In fact, I am sure if it were my first work, and other work was secondary, I would enjoy it. I know I've made other people think, and I've tried to make myself think that I dislike all household duties; but down in my secret heart I know it is untrue, and it has arisen from an idea that I really adopted "you can have everything you want, if you only don't want everything you can't have" and so long as I thought these duties were perhaps not for me, I tried not to want them, and have been very successful, for I took up so many other duties that they were quite crowded out of my work and often from my mind. And now that they have come to me, or will very soon, it troubles me somewhat to know if I should make them primary as it would please me to, or whether it is my duty to make them secondary to my other work, as I am now doing. At least, it seems to me the latter will be proper until another W. F. M. S. doctor has been here a year, and I think I can, and be happy about it too.

---

[22] Excerpts from the poem "God Knows" by Neil Randolph Blount.

Diary of Dr. Rosetta Hall 1892-1894

I have been getting the rooms down at the hospital fixed up for Miss Lewis. Had a new floor of narrow matched board put in the front room—the bedroom's floor covered with Korean oiled paper, and shelves and clothes hooks put up in a small room off of the bedroom which will make a nice clothes room, and will also be large enough for Pong Epie to have for her little room. We have planned for her to go down there to room when Miss Lewis does. She seems to love Miss Lewis very much, and Miss Lewis has a good influence over her. She is such a wild unruly girl. I shall be glad if something more can be done for her, for there is something in her. Have also had a small closet made outside for the commode. Everything now is ready, and as soon as it grows a little warmer, Miss Lewis will go down. She is fixing it up to suite her as the days go by, and will make it very pleasant and pretty. It has all come around right for her to go. I think no one would object now anyhow, but as Rev. Appenzeller commanded me not to allow it at one time, I asked and obtained his permission, and also Miss Rothweiler's. Of course when Mrs. Scranton and Miss Paine[23] the new teacher comes, the room will really be needed, and I imagine if Miss Lewis were not planning to go, she would get some hints that way now. Mrs. Scranton expected her to go there, so Miss Lewis brought word, and that went along ways in settling.

---

[23] Miss Josephine O. Paine (1869 – 1909) was appointed by W.F.M.S. to Korea in 1892 for educational work. Following Rothweiler, she served as the third principal of the Ewha Girls' School for 14 years. She died in 1909 and was interred at Yanghwajin Foreign Missionary Cemetery.

Diary of Dr. Rosetta Hall 1892-1894

We had a mail Saturday night. Everyone got a good mail, but I got no letters. I was much disappointed in not getting any letter from my mother. I had two little notes on the Advocate wrapped from her, one dated February 11 and one 22nd, and I am sure they must have gotten both Dr. Hall's and my letters about our upcoming marriage before that, and I don't understand why nothing was said about it. I waited so long for this mail, and now must wait another two weeks I fear, and then I don't know but that they have concluded to take no notice of our letters.

> "Do they think of me at Home
>   Do they ever think of me?
> I who shared their every grief
>   I who mingled in their glee
> I would give the world to know
>   'Do they think of me at Home.'
>
> Do they think of how I loved
>   In my home those happy days
> Do they think of him who came
>   But could never win their praise?
>
> Will no kind forgiving word
>   Come across the raging foam?
> I am happy by his side
>   And from mine he'll never roam
> But my heart will sadly ask,
>   'Do they think of me at Home?'"

A bit silly as most such songs are from which this quotation is made, but the sentiment sort of agrees with my mood tonight.

Diary of Dr. Rosetta Hall 1892-1894

Tuesday, April 12, 1892

Thou wilt keep him in perfect peace whose mind is stayed on Thee because He trusteth in Thee. Isa. xxvi. 3

"'What if they do go down?' said George MacDonald's godly woman, of her sons on the ocean. 'What's the bottom of the sea?' The answer came full and true, "the hollow of Hand.""

This is Esther's birthday, the 16th of the.[24] I wrote her a birthday letter, and gave her a memorial birthday text book. I have one for each of my Physiology class girls. Annie has had hers, as her birthday came first. They are quite neat, with spaces opposite the day and its text for people's autographs. Esther had a number of letters and little presents from the girls and women. I found some of her Korean candy on my table with this little note.

"My dear doctor, I give something to you, if you do not like to eat this, but take with my love. Will you, my faithful and affectionate doctor?"

It is six weeks now since my doctor went away. Last Thursday on my way to the class room, Rev. Appenzeller handed me a telegram which made me very happy. It said that the Doctor left 위쥬[25] Monday the 4th, so we expect him in Seoul by the 16th, Saturday. Rev. Jones will stay a few weeks longer. Dr. Hall comes back earlier so as to re-

---

[24] Esther Kim (born Chom Tong Kim, baptized Esther) was born on March 16, 1876 in lunar calendar and her birthday in 1892 fall on April 12th.
[25] Euiju. Rosetta spells in many different ways, "We Chu,""We Ju," "Wee Ju."

Diary of Dr. Rosetta Hall 1892-1894

lieve Dr. McGill who wishes to make a country trip to the East of Korea, starting next week. It will seem so good to see the Doctor again, yet now that I have heard from him, I think I could easily wait longer—but I confess for a week or two before that, the time did seem long. Miss Bengel and I think that some of the letters must have been lost, as we never received any from Pyong An and they must surely have written from there.[26] I asked Miss Bengel one day if she didn't think perhaps the Korean law had been executed upon them—decapitation for teaching Christianity, but she said I couldn't scare her that way. She is expecting a nice long letter with Dr. Hall from Mr. Jones so is looking forward to the Doctor's arrival quite as eagerly as I. We both promise when once married to be like John Wesley's wife, to scold, and make home so uncomfortable that our respective husbands will be glad to get off upon long itinerating trips to the country. But as yet we are not quite equal to that sacrifice of self, and we feel we have been pretty brave to endure our separation with as much grace as we have.

Have more dispensary patients now, 16 to 20 a day again. Have had some bad cases of mammitis[27]. One woman with the trouble in each breast, she is doing well. Yesterday, Miss Lewis helped me to get ready to amputate a thumb for necrosed bone, but the patient didn't turn up. Today we made arrangements for an ether operation in the morning for enlarged lymphatic glands of the neck on a

---

[26] Rosetta added later, "These letters came the next morning. They were written March 17th."
[27] Mastitis: inflammation of the breast.

Diary of Dr. Rosetta Hall 1892-1894

bright little girl the daughter of a *"yangban*[28].*"* We were quite sure of her, as her grandmother brought her today with bedding, rice and wood. I trust we may get along nicely, that she will do well, and that they may learn to love God and our dear Saviour, His Son, while with us. The little girl reads and seems such an interesting child.

No letters from home yet. The last American mail we sent home sunk with the Japanese steamer it was upon. I had sent $3 to Mrs. Jenkens for some silk lace for my wedding dress. Think I'll do without it now. We have not heard particulars of the trouble.

After Dispensary today, Miss Bengel and I called at the Russian legation, at Mrs. Chow's and upon Mrs. Gale. Last Thursday, Mrs. Heron became Mrs. Gale.[29] We met both Mr. and Mrs. Gale and the two children and they all seem very happy in their new Home ("The Folly")" but I believe they expect soon to move to Won San to open mission work there. Mr. Gale has joined the Presbyterian Mission. He seems very affectionate, and she looks younger and prettier, and I believe they are a loving couple, and probably as happy in each other as though she had not been married before. Think it must be all right, though when we first heard it was to be, it didn't seem quite right for Mr. Gale. Of

---

[28] The *yangban* were part of the traditional ruling class or nobles of dynastic Korea during the Joseon Dynasty.
[29] James S. Gale and Harriet Gibson (former Mrs. John. W. Heron) were married on April 7, 1892 at the British Consulate in Seoul and then had a wedding ceremony at the home of Mr. and Mrs. Gifford's, officiated by Mr. Ohlinger.

course she is doing well enough, but from all appearances this afternoon, would say that he is too.

> "Heaven causes marriages between those who have a recondite sympathy for each other, and brings them together." —From the Chinese

The character translated "recondite sympathy" may be translated as well "inexplicable attraction."

Tuesday, April 19, 1892

He that dwelleth in the secret place of the most High shall abide under the shadow of the Almighty. Psa. xci. 1

> It is faith, not feeling, leaning, not resolving, that carries us through. —Bonar

I did the operation last week as I expected to, and the little patient has done so nicely—has not had a temperature of 100° since. I redressed the wound today for the first since 24 hours after the operation, and found all in good condition, removed the suture—had union by first intention, except in the lower end of the wound where I left the silk ligature of occipital artery hanging out. If it had not been for this ligation, she would be practically well now, but will have to wait for that to slough off. I am almost sorry I didn't trust to a Catgut ligature[30], but the wounded artery was of good size and had but just

---

[30] Catgut ligature is a type of surgical suture that is naturally degraded by the body's own proteolytic enzymes.

Diary of Dr. Rosetta Hall 1892-1894

branched off of the carotid, and I feared secondary hemorrhage. The little one is just as good as she can be and Miss Lewis says it is a pleasure to look after her. The grandmother is growing quite interested in the Gospel Story, and studies away at her copy every day.

I have a from 20 to 25 patients per day now, get through by 4 p.m. unless there are a lot of cases to be irrigated and dressed antiseptically when it sometimes takes until 5 o'clock.

Rev. Appenzeller says he does like people to do as you expect them, and I think it is a satisfaction. We expected Dr. Hall in Saturday evening, and sure enough though he was stopped by the rain Thursday, he got in before 6 p.m. It is so good to know he is here again. He is quite well, was sick but once with a cold while gone. The sun and wind have done their work in browning him, and I think he looks a bit thinner, due to Korean chow, and hard walking I suppose. He walked 35 miles some days. The Doctor seems not at all disappointed with his first country trip, but rather quite encouraged. He treated [ ] and sold to them [ ]. As a result of the Evangelistic work up to the time Doctor left Rev. Jones, some 50 had been added to the church upon probation. He had many very interesting experiences, some hardships of course, but upon the whole was treated very kindly by the Korean people whom he feels sure may be won to Christ, though it will take much hard work and thorough consecration upon the part of God's children.

Monday, Dr. McGill came in to look at the orbital cavity in my skull. He and Dr. Hall wished to remove a tumor

Diary of Dr. Rosetta Hall 1892-1894

from that region. He also borrowed my Allis ether inhaler. He wanted to get off on his country trip today, but I don't know if he did.

Mrs. Vinton came in and spent most of Monday morning with me. We had a pleasant visit. My eyes are troubling me again, so it was a good thing I have something to keep me from studying or writing.

Miss Lewis has gotten moved down to the hospital and looks very nice there and seems perfectly contented. Just received a note from Doctor saying he feared he'd be late in coming this evening that Rev. Appenzeller wished his financial report. Said he "had been giving a little time to our garden today." "Our garden" strikes me a little strange as yet.

Doctor had quite a large mail awaiting him and he read me his letters. In one from Dr. Scranton was this little scrap which I am vain enough to be pleased with.

> "I trust Dr. Sherwood is long since quite well again. However much Korea may have disappointed you, I know you are not disappointed in her."

That was real nice and sweet of Dr. Scranton I am sure, and I wish I deserved it.

Diary of Dr. Rosetta Hall 1892-1894

Dr. William James Hall's letter, April 22, 1892:

> Friday 2.45 P.M.
>
> My dear Rosetta
>
> Will you please excuse me from the walk this afternoon?
>
> Not that I do not care to go as I look forward to being with you as one of the most desirable and enjoyable pleasures of each day.
>
> But as the mail goes out this evening at 5 o'clock I would like to get some letters ready.
>
> Would it be advisable or desirable for us to walk over to the post office together after tea?
>
> Thank you very much doctor for the first fruits of your violets. I forgot it last night.
>
> With much love
> Will.

Diary of Dr. Rosetta Hall 1892-1894

Friday 2:45 p.m.

My dear Rosetta,

Will you please excuse me from the walk this afternoon?

Not that I do not care to go as I look forward to being with you as one of the most desirable and enjoyable pleasures of each day. But as the mail goes out this evening at 9 o'clock I would like to get some letters ready.

Would it be advisable or desirable for us to walk over to the post office together after tea?

Thank you very much doctor for the first fruits of your violets. I forgot it last night.

With much love,
Will

Tuesday, April 26, 1892

But I will hope continually, and will yet praise Thee more and more. Psa. lxxi. 14

> His purposes will ripen fast
>   Unfolding every hour:
> The bud may have a bitter taste,
>   But sweet will be the flower.
> —Cowper[31]

My heart is so full of praise; I don't know where to begin to write.

Doctor has just gone, and as it is after 10 o'clock, and I have had a pretty hard day's work, I suppose I better go to

---

[31] William Cowper was a British poet and hymnist. This is an excerpt from his poem, "God Moves in Mysterious Ways."

Diary of Dr. Rosetta Hall 1892-1894

bed now, and if I get time, write later about the good mail which came, at last, yesterday. It was worth waiting for. It has been 5 weeks since I received any letters, but I can forget it now.

Dr. Hall and I each received the long looked for letter from Mother. Doctor got his mail first, and he gave me his letter. I will quote it in full.

Mr. Hall,

Yours of January 16th received. Rosetta knows how I feel in regard to her marrying. If you both think it is the Lord's doings we will call it right, for we all know He doeth all things well. We both give our consent to you to marry our daughter Rosetta, and hope and pray that your marriage may prove a very happy one, a long and useful one.

Mr. and Mrs. R. R. Sherwood

February 25, 1892.

Well, I felt pretty well pleased with that. Bless the dear mother-heart; I know it must have cost her much. In my letter she says, "The hardest thing I have ever written will be to answer Dr. Hall's letter."[32]

A few hours later my mail got arrived—Mother's usual fat letter of twelve pages, was the first to be devoured. Mother says, "Now my dear child, it is a hard job for me to

---

[32] Rosetta saved a clip she wrote in her diary, "Mother, your eldest daughter 'has gone the way of all girls who will not be advised by their mothers' (L. C. Rothweiler)."

Diary of Dr. Rosetta Hall 1892-1894

give you away to another for God knows I do love you, and this is something I never expected to be called upon to do. Your Pa and your Sister of course consent to it. As far as I am concerned, if you're always going to do missionary work and you love Dr. Hall as you say you do, I will call it for the best." But dear Mother has a very tender conscience, and it wouldn't let her off so easy after all. Later she writes, "Well, if you will believe it, I couldn't get to sleep last night, in fact, began to think I wouldn't sleep at all. I have made up my mind to give you my consent to marry your Doctor. Yesterday, I didn't think I would or could ever do this, but somehow or other, I couldn't get to sleep till I promised myself to put it down in black and white. Of course it will make you and the Doctor feel better and happier and myself also." "I wish you both ever so much joy and happiness, a long and useful life, and that God will bless the union to the good of you both, and that you may be great workers in His vineyard."

Dear Mother, I am sure I love you more than ever I could if I had not known that same doctor whom you are now willing to give me to. My heart was too narrow to half love you enough before, and I've no doubt that in the new experiences that lie before me I shall learn to love and appreciate you yet more.

When I think of Mother's feelings in regard to my marriage, I cannot help but to be reminded of the beautiful piece of poetry by Ella Wheeler Wilcox and entitled "The Mother-in-law." The last verse runs like this:

Diary of Dr. Rosetta Hall 1892-1894

"My pleasure in her joy is bitter sweet.
    Your very goodness sometimes hurts my heart,
Because, for her, life's drama seems complete
    Without the mother's oft-repeated part.
Be patient with me! She was mine so long
Who now is yours. One must indeed be strong,
    To meet the loss without the least regret.
And so, forgive me, if my eyes <u>are</u> wet."

Tuesday, May 17

I will bless the Lord at all times. Psa. xxxiv. 1

And why not? All is fulfilling His Word, which is the same as working out his love-plans for us.
—Margaret Bottome

The last two or three weeks have been unusually busy and anxious ones. First, beside my regular work, which with the fine weather is increasing now from 25 to 36 dispensary patients per day, Miss Bengel broke down in what I fear is rather a weak point with her. Two hours a day was spent in her treatment, and before she got quite well, Miss Lewis was taken very dangerously sick with rheumatic fever—temperature ranged from 103° to 106° for a week, and then suddenly fell from 105° to 98° in a few hours. I was with her and caught it at 101.8° and at once began to give stimulants, or I fear it would have gone down too low to ever come up again. For three days after she was very much prostrated, temperature often going down to 96.4° and we had to watch with her night and day. I had to be

Diary of Dr. Rosetta Hall 1892-1894

both doctor and nurse and if it had not been for Dr. Hall who helped me out several nights and shared the responsibility with me, I am sure I'd broken down myself, but now I am feeling quite rested again. Miss Lewis is growing a bit stronger every day now, and will soon be able to sit up. Oh, I know not how to be thankful enough, for 36 hours or more I so feared we could not keep her with us, but praise the Lord, He let her remain, and I am sure it is not for naught.

With all the other work, my tailor came last week and began my little bridal outfit. I verily believe I shall not have time to get married after all when the day comes. I could spend so little time in the fitting and supervision of the work that I haven't even try wedding dress to fit nicely or to look just as I'd like it too. Well, I can be thankful that I have any at all. Don't know what I would have, if in Japan I have not happened to buy a piece of white Japanese silk thinking I'd have it for an evening dress, but have never had time to get it made up before, so now it comes in very good. It is a nice piece and I think will look pretty well made up with a full plain skirt, and a basque with a bit of embroidered silk crepe in a point front and back—the silk laid in three folds on either side. I'd like a plainer basque, but on account on my deformity cannot well wear one unless it be made of plush or heavy cloth.

Doctor is busy with Dr. McGill's work, and the language, and I am busy with mine, so that we don't get much time for walks these beautiful days. At few times we have gone out in the evening, when we have been disappointed in not being able to get out through the day. I ought to get out

Diary of Dr. Rosetta Hall 1892-1894

every day. The fresh air does me so much good. How much I enjoy my doctor's company—more and more, as a days go by. I wonder now how I could ever have been quite happy without him.

> "My thoughts are like the little birds,
>   Your heart is like the nest;
> They rove the sky on fearless wings,
>   To you they come for rest,
> Well-knowing, though the world be fair,
>   Your tender love is best.
>
> My songs are like the little streams,
>   Your heart is like the sea;
> Though through the woods they wander on
>   So careless, glad, and free,
> They seek at last the silent deep —
>   They come at last to thee."
> —Grace H. Duffield

Diary of Dr. Rosetta Hall 1892-1894

Letter from Dr. William James Hall:

Dr. Sherwood

My dear Rosetta,

Thank you very much for making out the schedule. I am afraid I am asking you to do too much along with your other work. I will be up to see you in a few minutes, unless you are busy. If so, please let me know.

With much love,

Will

Diary of Dr. Rosetta Hall 1892-1894

June 1, 1892

He that will love life and see good days, let him refrain his tongue from evil and his lips that they speak no guile, let him eschew evil and do good, let him seek peace and ensue it. I Pet. 3:10,11

> "And what is so rare as a day in June?
> Then, if ever, come perfect days;
> Then Heaven tries earth if it be in tune,
> And over it softly her warm ear lays;
> Whether we look, or whether we listen,
> We hear life murmur, or see it glisten;"
> —James Russell Lowell

I suppose from henceforth June is to be a memorable month to me. I always did love June, but now it seems sweeter than ever. Why?

Sunday, June 26 — This has been such an extremely busy month. I have not had opportunity to write in my journal. I am sorry too, as there have been many things I should liked to have recorded. Just 6 months ago tonight, Sunday, December 27, the dear Lord put into my heart the desire which will be recognized formerly, in the morning, by both the civil and ecclesiastic marriage ceremony.

Monday, June 27, 1892, Wedding Day

I will bring the blind by a way that they know not; I will lead them in paths that they had not known. I will make darkness light before them, and crooked things straight.

Diary of Dr. Rosetta Hall 1892-1894

These things will I do unto them, and not forsake them. Isa. xlii. 16

> Marriage is honorable in all. Heb. 13:4
>
> "True Love is but a humble, low-born thing,
> And hath its food served up in earthen ware;
> It is a thing to walk with, hand in hand,
> Through the everydayness of this workday world."
> —James Russell Lowell

Between the Acts: 10:30 a.m. — At 9 o'clock Doctor and I, accompanied by Dr. and Mrs. Scranton, Rev. Jones and Miss Bengel, went over to the British Legation and were married by His Britannic Majesty's Consul Walter C. Hillier. This marriage is legal anywhere within British rule, but to be legal in the U.S. it must be repeated before the American Consul which will be done at 12 noon.

12 noon. — Rev. Ohlinger assisted by Rev. Bunker performed the Ecclesiastical Ceremony in the presence of Dr. Horace N. Allen, U.S. Deputy Consul General.

It is a glorious June day. Everything and everybody seem happy, including the bridegroom and bride.

Mrs. M. F. Scranton assisted by Misses Bengel and Lewis have made preparations for a fine wedding before some 35 or 40 invited guests, and our Korean house people.

I have everything all packed, except taking off my wedding dress to put in the trunk and we are going to try to get

Diary of Dr. Rosetta Hall 1892-1894

off for Chemulpo by 2 p.m. to take the *Genkai* for Chefoo early in the morning.

So far, I am not a bit nervous, and feel real well in spite of the fact that an old mosquito kept me awoke most of the night by getting under my net.

I do thank God with all my heart for the way in which He is leading, and for the peace and joy and trustfulness that fills my heart.

I must now dress for the second act. I wore a simple muslin dress in the first, plain full skirt gathered upon a round waist with some handmade lace in neck and sleeves that sister Maggie[33] sent to me last Christmas. For the second act I have a pretty white silk dress. Then I shall don my travelling dress of drab and white (straight skirt and blouse waste) and tennis cap. I shall be so relieved when all the form and ceremony is through with, though I am not minding it so much as I feared I might.

I wonder if the folks at Home are thinking about me today.

Well, it is all through now. The religious ceremony seemed much the more solemn and impressive, even though we did have to kiss the Bible as in the civil ceremony. What impressed both Doctor and myself the most was the expression, "I pronounce you husband and wife." We had a real pleasant time with the friends present and en-

---

[33] Mrs. Margaret Ver Noy Sherwood is Rosetta's brother Charles Hurd Sherwood's wife.

Diary of Dr. Rosetta Hall 1892-1894

joyed the refreshments that were served with such bounty. I slipped out about 1 o'clock and the Doctor came after, and we were on our journey to Chemulpo by 2 p.m. Started off amid showers of rice and good wishes. It was the most pleasant trip down I have taken yet. The weather was delightful, and the rice fields are looking so green with waving fields of yellow barley here and there.

Doctor seemed quite set back to former days. He walked by my chair or we walked together some of the time. Later in the evening as he rode along horseback he sang me many old songs that mother used to sing, and made me quite homesick. Many times he expressed his joy and pleasure in what had taken place today. He thinks God is so good to him. Well, I am glad he is happy, and I am quite as sure that God is good to me. I have more to praise Him for than the Doctor, it seems to me.

We did not reach Chemulpo till after 11 p.m. The *Genkai* was not in so we went to Steward's Hotel. We secured a small room which had two beds in it, and after reading the 23rd Psalm and having prayer together we retired. I rested nicely but was not able to sleep much, neither was the Doctor. He was so kind and good, and loving to me. I love him more than ever, and am beginning to realize a bit that we are indeed "husband-and-wife." Another beautiful day has dawned upon us, so if there is anything in the old adage about days we ought to prove to be a good husband and wife, and with our Father's help, we will. Oh, I am so glad that Doctor is such a perfect child of God, he is such a help to me. Our natures are quite different in a few

Diary of Dr. Rosetta Hall 1892-1894

respects, but one will only serve to balance the other, we trust.

I am tempted to quote still farther from Lowell on Love, where he speaks of

> "A love that in its object findeth not
> All grace and beauty, and enough to sate
> Its thirst of blessing, but, in all of good
> Found there, it sees but Heaven-granted types
> Of good and beauty in the soul of men
> And traces, in the simplest heart that beats,
> A family likeness to its chosen one,
> That claims of it the rights of brother hood."
> —Lowell

I believe that something like this applies to both Doctor's love and my own, and I am glad it is so; as rich and as sweet as our love is, incomplete without Him who first loved us.

Wednesday, June 29, 1892

As thy days, so shall thy strength be. Deut. xxxiii. 25

> "Like a cradle, rocking, rocking,
>   Silent, peaceful, to and fro,
> Like a mother's sweet looks dropping
>   On the little face below,
> Hangs the green earth, swinging, turning,
>   Jarless, noiseless, safe and slow;
> Falls the light of God's face, bending,
>   Down and watching us below."[34]

---

[34] From "The Love of God" by Helen Hunt Jackson (1830-1885). Beside "Saxe Holm," she used "H.H." and "Rip van Winkle" as other pseudonyms for publications.

Diary of Dr. Rosetta Hall 1892-1894

Another beautiful day. We are still at Steward's. The *Genkai* is late. (Captain Thompson made his fog[35], but also, we didn't know for sure that he could, so we had to be married upon Monday and hurry down here all the same.)

They just now tell me the *Genkai* is in sight. I am glad, because of course it is much pleasant to be at Chefoo than here—yet we are very happy here. Dear Doctor is so good, so thoughtful for my comfort. I am sort of a matter of fact person and never built very high castles upon the joys and comfort of married life; but so far I think much more than my highest hopes are being realized.

The *Genkai* came in at noon, and we went abroad about 5 p.m. Are to sail at 3 a.m. We had a good night. The state-rooms upon the *Genkai* are the best any I ever saw. There are two good sized windows instead of port holes, and as the rooms and dining room are all on deck, the windows do not have to be closed. There is every convenience in our state-rooms and all in such small compass, that it seemed as if there was more space left than in our room at Steward's Hotel.

We, neither of us felt a bit seasick in the morning, and enjoyed our breakfast, but before tiffin Doctor felt badly, and about 3 p.m., I began to pay my usual contributions to the Yellow Sea. I was not so sick this time as when I went over last year however. But my poor Doctor, before he

---

[35] Likely referring to how Captain James Thompson (1821-?) was able to recruit the Independent Battery C unit of the Pennsylvania Light Artillery (known as Thompson's Battery C) during the American Civil War.

Diary of Dr. Rosetta Hall 1892-1894

gave up and got into his berth, he was so sick that it would not have mattered just then if the ship had gone down so long as it would take him with her. It grew quieter, however, later, and we both slept some and passed a fair night, and found ourselves at Chefoo in the morning.

We have just the room at the Sea View Hotel that we wanted, the one the McKenzies had last year. We are very comfortable indeed here, and I am sure our vacation will do us good. Doctor hired a boat for a month, and we have been out rowing already the first day of our arrival.

Monday, July 4, 1892

Come ye yourselves apart, and rest a while. Mark vi. 31

Water rests only when it gets to the lowest place. So do men. —Drummond

Here is the "Glorious Fourth" once more. Our landlady secured some American flags, and very kindly put one up over the stone arch to our door, but they tell me that after all I am not now an American anymore. I said to the Doctor, "But what am I?" "A British subject," was the answer, but I think I will never forget that I was born a free American citizen; and I can't yet fully realize that I am not now, though it has come to me with more force today than ever before.

However, American or British as it may be, I do know I am happier than ever before. It all seems too sweet to last,

Diary of Dr. Rosetta Hall 1892-1894

but I am so glad that Doctor always looks upon the bright side of things. He expects the good, and it comes. It is said we always find what we look for, but I can truly say I am finding much more than looked for. Doctor says "Praise the Lord" and I say "Amen."

We have been married one week today. We are very staid and proper in public and no strangers imagine us so recently married, but in the privacy of our own room (where the Doctor prefers to keep me the most of the time) he makes love to me like the simple-hearted boy that he is. The idea of the Rev. W. J. Hall, M.D. calling me his "dearest darling," and kissing me until I have to frighten him by saying "someone will see you," I would never have believed it. He had a good one on me though a bit ago. He came near me, and as that has grown to be almost an established signal to me to expect a kiss, I prepare to receive it, but he was only on his way to wash his face. Catching my attitude and expression, he wished for a Kodak and we both laughed until the tears rolled down our cheeks. But our love is not all so silly as the above might seem to warrant. Strange though, there seems to be no radically different way for love to be expressed. Shallow youth and mature manhood have both to use much the same vocabulary in word and action, but there is an earnestness, a depth of feeling, in the latter that one cannot help but to know that neither the words nor the actions half express. "Thought is deeper than all speech, feeling deeper than all thought, souls to souls can never teach, what unto themselves was

Diary of Dr. Rosetta Hall 1892-1894

taught."[36] It is in prayer that the Doctor best expresses himself. He is never done praising the dear Master for bringing us together.

Day by day am I getting fresh glimpses of how much the dear Lord Jesus must love His bride, the church, and I do want to love Him with my whole soul, and to please him in everything that comes to my hand to do; but my lips seem dumb, and my hands paralyzed when I think of how very little after I can do in comparison for what He has done and is doing for me.

> "I feel as weak as a violet
> Alone 'neath the awful sky
> Winds wander, and dews drip earthward,
> Rain falls, suns rise and set,
> Earth whirls; and all but to prosper
> A poor little violet!"[37]

I often feel much the same toward my Doctor, I want to show him by word or action something of how much I love him, and it seems so easy and natural at first, but the feeling put in thought grows colder, and when I try to put it into words they freeze up on my lips. Why is this? I think I am too proud, I can't bear to express the deep and sacred thoughts of my heart in the same words that are so often used foolishly. I must get over this pride. It is the bane of my life, and I can't help to make the lives of those I love half so happy as I otherwise could. I am not where my quo-

---

[36] Christopher Pearse Cranch (1813–1892). Rosetta's teacher wrote this quotation on her book when she was young. See November 23, 1890 diary.
[37] "The Changeling" by James Russell Lowell.

tation for the day suggests as the place to find rest. Dear Lord, I want to loose all of this pride. I want to be willing to be, to do, or to say the most humble thing that will serve to bring joy to Thee or to one of Thy creatures.

We have received the congratulations from Mr. and Mrs. Appenzeller written from The Oriental Hotel, Kobe as follows,

> "Dear Dr. and Mrs. Hall,
> Hearty congratulations! Long and many years of usefulness and happiness! I believe Jesus was present at the 'marriage' in Seoul of Korea because 'both Jesus was called, and his disciples, to the marriage.'[38] May God bless you richly in all things, both temporal and spiritual is the wish and prayer of your friends.
> The Appenzellers"

Isn't that lovely? I can't tell how much I appreciate it.

Dear Miss Rothweiler also left a note to be given me after marriage. She says, "Most fully and heartily do I say: God bless you both and give to you prosperity, happiness and health in a beautiful measure, and may He grant that you both maybe the means of bringing blessings to many others."

---

[38] John 2:2.

Diary of Dr. Rosetta Hall 1892-1894

Monday, July 25, 1892

Not as though I had already attained, either were already perfect; but I follow after, if that I may apprehend that for which also I am apprehended of Christ Jesus. Phil. iii. 12

> The child opens his eyes upon the wonder of the world, and comes to a knowledge of his powers little by little. In myself, I was never more a child, never more on the threshold of all possible good, than I am today. ++ The power to comprehend only reveals more and more to comprehend. The power to enjoy but reveals more and more to enjoy. ++ Slowly, by toil and pain, there has come to me a more sacred friendship, a deeper worship, a vaster thought, a more abundant delight. If this may continue; if the way may still conduct me into higher sensations, into greater knowledge, into more divine love; if the future shall open and open; ++ if I may draw closer to better hearts, and draw out more of the fathomlessness of my being; if this may be, just this, step-by-step, little by little, — I shall not ask, for I cannot conceive, a more glorious destiny.
> —Herman Bisbee

Today, at the end of our first moon of wedded life, I know not how better to express my thoughts and feelings than by the above, except perhaps I would omit the signs of the subjective mood, and change to the simple future tense.

Diary of Dr. Rosetta Hall 1892-1894

We have had such a joyous month, and it has passed by so quickly that I can not at all think it was four whole weeks ago that we were married.

Rev. Gifford and wife, Dr. and Mrs. Brown, and Mrs. Bunker came upon the last steamer, and Rev. Bunker and Dr. Vinton came upon the next. They all will remain until September. Mrs. Greathouse returns with us August 4th upon the *Genkai*.

We spend our mornings mostly in writing, taking a sea-bath after 11 o'clock which generally makes me feel cool and comfortable the rest of the day. I do not learn to swim, think I am a great coward about it than last year. Nearly every evening if not too rough we get out in the boat, I have made some progress here—can manage one bar pretty well and am beginning to get up enough muscle for two. We always take some of the Seoulites, or Mr. and Mrs. McKee or five little boys, with us as it is quite a good sized boat, and Doctor is never quite so happy as when he is giving all the pleasure he can to the most number of people.

Today the American mail came. There was none for Doctor, but I had my usual 12 pages from Mother written from May 24 to June 3rd. All are well, praise the Lord. I also had a letter from Miss Platt[39], and some papers, and nice long letters from Mrs. Scranton, Miss Bengel and Miss Lewis, and a little one from Pong Sunie.

---

[39] Miss Platt from New York, one of the women "who left the Deaconess Home of New York on account of the bonnet." Refer to Rosetta's diary of July 24, 1981.

Diary of Dr. Rosetta Hall 1892-1894

> Seoul Korea
> July 4, 1892
>
> My very dear and faithful friend Dr.
> I hope you are well and happy, we are all well, are you glad because you stay with Dr. Hall. you like there? there time we have not much patience, we three girls and my mother come drug room and see these patience. I wish to see you very much do you wish to see us. I wanted tell you some thing. thank you very much because you give me your picture I like very much. I see your picture every day but I want talk with you that in only picture can not talk with the picture. I am afraid you forget me, I don't forget you. I hope you are peaceful heart, always I pray for you & I hope God

> bless you every where you life. my mother said she is very sorry because she can not see you when you go 미국. If she know how can write letter then she write but she can't I hope you come back soon. I wanted write long letter but I have no time to write long letter.
>
> your sincerely Friend
> Pong Sunie
>
> To From Seoul Korea
> R S Hall

Letter from Ponsunie

57

Diary of Dr. Rosetta Hall 1892-1894

Seoul, Korea
July 4, 1892

R.S. Hall

My very dear and faithful friend, Doctor—

I hope you are well and happy. We are all well. Are you glad because you stay with Dr. Hall? You like there? These time, we have not much patients. We three girls and my mother come drug room and see these patients. I wish to see you very much. Do you wish to see me? I wanted tell you something. Thank you very much because you give me your picture. I like very much. I see your picture every day but I want talk with you. That is only picture. Cannot talk with the picture. I'm afraid you forget me. I don't forget you. I hope you are peaceful heart always. I pray for you and I hope God bless you everywhere you live. My mother said she is very sorry because she cannot see you when you go 치푸 [Chefoo]. If she know how read and write letter then she write but she can't. I hope you come back soon. I wanted write long letter but I have no time to write long letter.

Yours sincerely Friend,

Pong Sunie

Monday, August 1— We are now beginning to think of turning our faces homeward. We have had such a pleasant stay in Chefoo, meeting so many missionaries that are thoroughly consecrated has added much to our pleasure.

Diary of Dr. Rosetta Hall 1892-1894

We have met in prayer meeting each week beside the Sunday service, and then have called upon each other, taken tea and supper together, etc. One day we were invited to Dr. Randall's at Tong Shin of C. I. M. He was a friend of Doctor's in college in New York and I met the family here last summer so it was very pleasant for us all. We spent some of the time with the doctor in his dispensary and hospital. Saw a bound-footed woman remove her bandage for the doctor. She had walked 4 miles to get medicine for her husband on those poor little stumps of feet. The toes are all turned under except the great toe and at first sight they look as if they had all grown to each other laterally and posteriorly to the sole of the foot, but I found they could be lifted up. Then the great toe and heel are bent toward each other so as to shorten the foot as much as possible. Dr. Randall said the bones of the ankle are often dislocated this way. It is not very often one has the pleasure (?) of seeing such a foot. The Chinese women are very averse to showing them, but this poor woman had walked so far she complained of pain in feet and legs and as we were very anxious to see such a foot, Dr. Randall succeeded in getting her to unbind them while he applied Iodine.

Another day we were invited to supper at Dr. Corbett's of Presbyterian Mission. Rev. Mr. Goforth and wife and Miss McIntosh of Hunan Province of whom I heard the McKenzies speak often last year were also invited. These with Mrs. Corbett and Dr. Hall are all Canadians.

Another day we took tiffin at the sanatorium with Mr. and Mrs. Stook. They are such fine people. Of course here

Diary of Dr. Rosetta Hall 1892-1894

we met many of the C. I. M. people, many of whom come here from the interior for their health.

We took tea one afternoon with Miss Sanderson, the principle of the Girl's School C. I. M. She is a lady I admire very much. I met her last summer first. Doctor likes her so much also.

[Unidentified photo] Probably Sanitarium at Chefoo

Tuesday, August 2 — This morning Doctor, Mrs. Vinton, and I took a sampan and went out to the *Satsuma Maru* which had just come in harbor with Dr. and Mrs. McGill and family on board taking the round trip to Vladivostok and Shanghai. The Doctor had already gone ashore he ate Tiffin with us later. We had a nice visit with Mrs. McGill and the babies. They have had a very good time.

Diary of Dr. Rosetta Hall 1892-1894

Thursday, August 4 — Left on the *Genkai* at 9 a.m. for Korea. Mrs. Greathouse is pretty sick, but it seems wisest to all to get her home as soon as possible. We had a beautiful passage. After attending to Mrs. Greathouse this evening, I felt a little sick—that I'd soon have to make my usual contribution to Dame Ocean, but Doctor made me lie down at once and not lift my head again, he undressed me like a mother would her baby, and after a bit I feel better, went to sleep and rested well. Doctor also avoided being sick of any consequence upon this voyage, I am so glad. Reached Chemulpo, August 5, Friday noon. We made preparations to go up to Seoul at once, but when General Greathouse came down, he wished us to stay with his mother and go up on the little steamer Tuesday or Wednesday, which we did, reaching "home" at last Wednesday evening, August 10th.

Returning to Korea on *Genkai Maru*, August 4, 1892

Diary of Dr. Rosetta Hall 1892-1894

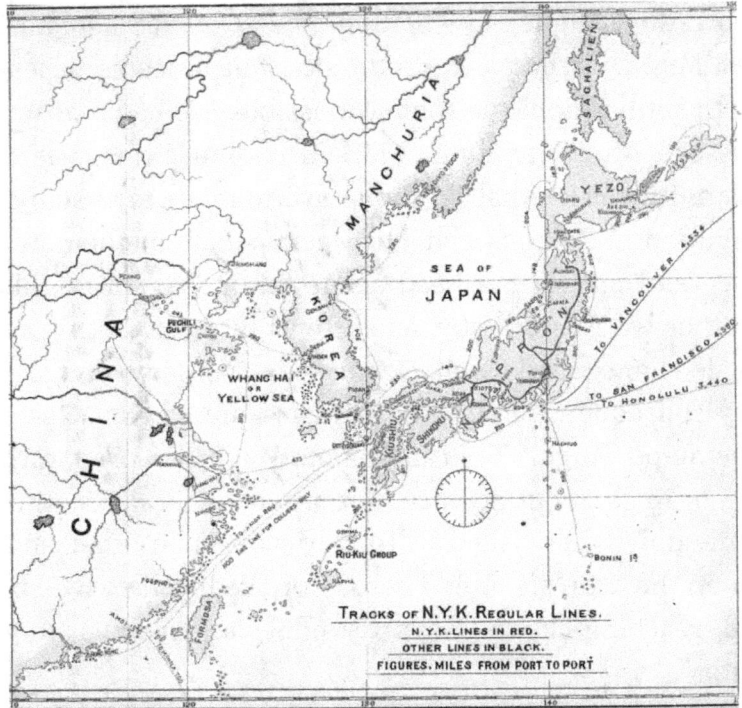

Voyage back from Chefoo to Korea on *Genkai Maru*, August 4, 1892

Monday, September 19, 1892

Everyone loveth gifts, and followeth after rewards. Isa. i. 23

> God's love gives in such a way that it flows from a Father's heart, the wellspring of all good. The heart of the giver makes the gift dear and precious; as among ourselves we say of even a trifling gift, "it comes from a hand we love," and look not so much at the gift as at the heart. —Luther

Diary of Dr. Rosetta Hall 1892-1894

Before I arose this morning, birthday remembrances began to come in, and before the day closed I had much more than I deserved. Miss Bengel sent me a table bell, Miss Lewis sent Miss Havergal's *My King* and a nice little note, Miss Paine a very pretty dish, Esther and "Emmagene" each a birthday letter; and Doctor signed over his life assurances to me—some $4000.

It has been a busy day. Doctor is preparing to go on a trip to the 평양 [Pyong Yang] Circuit that Bishop Mallalieu[40] appointed him to. He wants to get off tomorrow or next day if he can get ready. He has been working very hard. We expect Rev. Noble and wife this month, and it seems best that they should live with us; so Doctor has had move out all Rev. Appenzeller's things from the front room that they might have it for their sitting room and study, and moved our kitchen, repapering and fixing up the old one for their bedroom. Besides, Doctor has put up three stoves, fixed the leaks in the roof and a number of other things to leave us comfortable. Doctor persisted in having no one but our own servants to help him in all this, and he had charge of Dr. Scranton's hospital at the same time, and I must confess he got through with the such an amount of work in much less time than I thought possible. I have helped him amputate two fingers at the hospital recently. Doctor tells me so often how glad he is that I am a doctor; he seems to prefer it to any or all other accomplishments.

---

[40] Willard Francis Mallalieu (December 11, 1828 - August 1, 1911) was an American Bishop of the Methodist Episcopal Church, elected in 1884

Diary of Dr. Rosetta Hall 1892-1894

It is a very good thing that he does, for it is precious little beside that I'm good for, and I am not much good in that.

Today we have been married twelve weeks—three months! And have been "keeping house" one half that time.

> "Married and settled! Just look at the wife
> Deep in her newly fledged duties;
> Life ne'er before to her loving young heart
> Seemed quite so full of new beauties."

There is so much crowded into each day that makes life beautiful that I hardly know where to begin or how to end. The dear Lord is so good to me; the Holy Spirit is drawing me nearer to Him, and teaching me how I can better please Jesus, my Savior. I am a dull pupil, and my progress is very slow, but I am in the "School of Christ," and I am very happy there. Doctor is such a help to me, both by precept and example. I am sure I can advance further with him than I ever could have done without, and oh, how I do praise the Lord for such a husband.

In contemplation of the future, he would exclaim,
"It is glorious to live in these times and
be able to do something for Jesus."[41]

---

[41] A little note written by Rosetta, describing Dr. Hall's quotation.

Diary of Dr. Rosetta Hall 1892-1894

Our separation for the next four or five weeks will be very hard for both, but it is to help to bring Korea to Christ, and that is what we both came here for. At the Annual Mission Meeting held here, Bishop Mallalieu read the appointments September 5th, and while my work is to continue as a physician in the Woman's Hospital at Seoul, much to my surprise Dr. Hall was appointed to Pyong Yang (!), some 176 miles distant, to be there most of the time except through the coldest months and the rainy season. In Doctor's report[42], he had strongly recommended opening work in Pyong Yang, and offered to become responsible for one-half of the salary for a doctor sent to that field, but we scarcely thought it would be opened regularly until after the arrival of Doctor's friend Dr. Busteed[43], whom the Mission unanimously voted the Home Board to send out at the earliest opportunity. However, it is all right we feel sure, though it does look hard now, but surely the Lord is with us. He goes before.

---

[42] "The doors are wide open to the medical missionary in any of the northern cities through which we passed. They are pleading for us to send them a doctor. There would not be the slightest opposition to his residing in Pyong Yang or Wee Chu. Let us put a doctor thoroughly consecrated to God and filled with the Holy Ghost into Pyong Yang, and it will do more to open up our way for work into the northern interior than any other method we can adopt. If a doctor is placed in Pyong Yang I will become responsible for one half his salaray for two years." Excerpt from the Seventy-fourth Annunal Report of the Missionary Society of the Methodist Episcopal Church for the Year 1893, p 292.

[43] Dr. John B. Busteed arrived in Korea 1893 and did medical work at Si Pyung Won, the General Hospital, in Seoul. The Halls and the Nobles shared house to save money to support Dr. Busteed's coming to Korea. Dr. Busteed returned to New York in 1897 due to illness and died in 1901.

Diary of Dr. Rosetta Hall 1892-1894

In the mail today, Doctor got such a nice letter from Dr. Toy of Siam, congratulating him upon his marriage and speaking of the happiness to be derived from the same. I received no letter from —did not last mail either, but I had a short letter from my mother-in-law[44]. I wonder if she can understand what a loving husband her eldest boy makes. It does seem as if his love became stronger and stronger each day. He says he is going to court me all his life, and I believe he will. He makes more love to me now in one day than in a whole year before marriage. I thought our "honeymoon" very sweet, but it cannot compare with our "home life" now; and so our love goes on increasing as our hearts widen. Oh, how I love my Doctor, it seems as if I could never be with him quite enough.

> "Married and settled! Not bothered for gold!
> Mated! Not bound with a tether
> Hateful and irksome as chains to a slave,
> But, living in loving together!"

Wednesday, October 5, 1892

Do all to the glory of God. I Cor. x. 31

> "Moment by moment let down from Heaven,
> Time, opportunity, guidance are given;
> Fear not tomorrow, child of the King,
> Trust them to Jesus, do the next thing."

---

[44] Mrs. Margaret Bolton Hall.

Diary of Dr. Rosetta Hall 1892-1894

A beautiful day. It is a Korean holiday[45], at least in the sense that most work stops, and the people go out to offer sacrifice at the graves of their ancestors.

As there were not likely to be any patients at the hospital, I decided to give my "staff" a holiday, and take one myself. The Misses Paine and Lewis, and I at first planned to go out horseback-riding, but failing to get horses, we went in chairs quite a ways out in the country in the direction of "Ioge."[46] Many graves cover the hills lying about this road, and we saw a great number of people, mostly men and children, but some woman, all about, over these hills particularly in the ceremonies of the day. We heard much "howling" and some real weeping.

Thinking it would be interesting to watch at least one such rite from the beginning, we followed a closed chair carried by two coolies, with a woman servant behind bearing a load upon her head.

Some distance from the road, over on a hillside, the chairs stopped, and a lady got out, after searching about among the many round mounded graves, that look like hay-cocks in the distance, she evidently found the grave of her search. How they know or remember is more than I can tell, for there seems to be nothing marking the graves. We withdrew at a respectful distance and watched the proceedings. First the servant went and brought some water, then the lady washed all the dishes, some of which

---

[45] *Chuseok*, Korean Thanksgiving Day (August 15th in the lunar calendar).
[46] *Aogi* or *Aeogae* ("small ridge"), Ahyun-dong, Seoul.

were Japanese, and I noticed a foreign knife, then she prepared all the food carefully placing it in the dishes herself, the servant only waiting upon her a little. There was the bowl of rice, something that looked like pancakes, dumplings, honey, wine, pears, persimmons and green prunes. After arranging everything in order upon a tray, the lady covered it with an oiled paper, and gave it to the servant who placed it upon top of the grave, and then uncovered it. The lady then bowed herself at the side of the grave and began moaning and crying, and apparently praying. After some ten or fifteen minutes, she stopped, and then she and the servant began dividing the food which she had just offered in sacrifice between the chair coolies and the men who cleaned off the dead grass from the grave, and some children, boys who evidently go out this day in order to get these treats. Noticing me standing near, the lady politely asked me to come and sit down by her. I went. She offered me some of the food, but I declined. I asked her if she did not eat any, and she said no, it would not be right for her to. I asked her if it was her husband who was dead, though I scarcely thought it could be so she wore a silver pin in her hair. She said no, it was her mother and father. She told me she had never seen an American woman before. I told I was a doctor, and I invited to her to come to my dispensary sometime. She seemed like a nice honest hearted woman, and how I longed to be able to talk more to her. I was so sorry I had not even thought to bring any Christian Korean literature with me. Another year I would like to make it a point to do this.

Diary of Dr. Rosetta Hall 1892-1894

Later we found a nice shady grave where we ate our lunch in a little after noon. We were hungry and it tasted very good, though we were surrounded by I would say a hundred boys and men eagerly watching each movement. What was left we divided with them, and each seemed to enjoy getting a bite of foreign food. Then again we wished for a Gospel in Korean to ask one of them to read from, or if we had only some of our Korean Hymns so that Miss Lewis could have sung, it would have been such a nice opportunity of sowing a little seed for the Master. Well, it serves us a lesson for next time. The children picked us a lot of wildflowers, mostly white daisies, just like our home daisies, the first I had seen in Korea.

Among the crowd, there was one nice-looking man that Quen Sikie asked me if I did not remember; and I did. He was the uncle of the young woman who a year ago the last rainy season got cut over the breast and upon one leg by some falling tiles. I dressed the wounds a number of times, and she quite recovered, and he asked to pay the bill which he did, and made the hospital a nice present of paper besides. He lived in Seoul then, but I found had now moved outside, and lived near where we were, and he invited us to come to his house, saying his wife would be glad to see us. We went, and indeed she was glad. We had a nice little visit, and then started for home getting there before 3 o'clock. It was prayer meeting afternoon and Miss Lewis was to lead so we wished to get back in good time.

We had a good meeting at Mrs. McGill's. The Presbyterian ladies were about all out, but none of the Methodist except Miss Lewis and myself.

Diary of Dr. Rosetta Hall 1892-1894

My dear Doctor has been away two weeks today and I have not heard a word from him yet. I can't say that I am lonesome for I am too busy for that, but oh, I do miss him so much. I am homesick for him. I think that expresses it about as near as I can. I do so long to hear from him.

Monday, October 17, 1892

Be not over-anxious; but in everything by prayer and supplication with thanksgiving let your request be made known unto God. And the peace of God, which passeth all understanding, shall guard your hearts and minds through Christ Jesus. Phil. Iv. 6,7 R.V.

> "And now I pray for love, deep love to God and man,
> A love that will not fail, however dark His plan;
> That sees all life in Him, rejoicing in His power
> And faithful though the darkest clouds of gloom and doubt may lower,
> And God is kinder than my prayer
> Love fills and blesses everywhere."[47]

The very next morning after I wrote the paragraph upon the preceding page, I received such a good letter from Doctor. He sent it to me just a week from the time he left, and had written in it each day up to that time. I was delighted; and now today I have another, which he says is the third he has written, the second I've not yet received but hope to now at any time. Doctor says he is real well, has not been the least bit sick, my canvas steamer chair which

---

[47] From "For Sight, For Love" by Ednah Dow Cheney (1824-1904).

he took with him for a bed protects him from fleas and bugs—they liking the warm kang floors better—and the steamer with two apartments that he had made to use over a charcoal *wharrow*[48] works nicely, and he enjoys his meals though he took but very little foreign food with him. He studies Korean in the morning and sees patients in the afternoon. He writes that the prospects are good for a grand work, and he says nothing about ever coming back.

It seems a bit novel to me to be addressed as "My darling wife," but I rather like it, and I am sure that my doctor is just one of the dearest husbands in the world. I wish I could tell him how much I love him; and yet I am glad that it is impossible for words to measure it. Dear Doctor, here is a little glimpse of his great loving heart that I want to keep.

> "I have felt very lonely without you, darling. But I have sought special grace from the Master, and He is very precious to me. He has given me a heart to love and He comes in and fills it."

Praise the Lord.

Though I try to allow household duties to rest but lightly upon me, yet between them and the hospital I get very little time to study Korean, and less yet to read or write. In Mr. Appenzeller's library here, there are a number of books that if I could have had access to ten years ago as I have would not have remained many weeks unread. There

---

[48] A fire bowl. It is a heatproof container designed to hold charcoal, similar to a Japanese hibachi.

Diary of Dr. Rosetta Hall 1892-1894

are Hawthorne's that I used to want to read so much, and Alice and Phoebe Cary's poems and several others that would have delighted my heart, and how much I would like to read them now, but must forego.

I have of late been dipping into one book which I have desired to read ever since it was published, and that is Frances E. Willard's *Glimpses of Fifty Years* and it just fascinates me. I don't dare pick it up more than once or twice a week, for I never know when to lay it down again. Miss Willard has surely carried out Emerson's advice: "Say honestly and simply that which your own experience has given you, and you will give to the world something new, valuable, and lasting."

There is more than one uplift that I am much in need of I know, but just now I am thinking of how low down I am in a literary sense. I wish I might be pulled out of the rut I am in. I don't know that I ever did have any original thoughts, but it seems to me I do not even have commonplace thoughts anymore. I believe I do not really think at all. My time seems all taken up with a round of small duties, the doing of which leaves but little time to even think about them, let alone anything a little foreign to them. However, I firmly believe I am in my own little niche, and the work I am doing there is no one else to do at present. "If you want to serve your race go where no one else will go, and do what no one else will do."[49] This I remember to have read when quite a child, and I have often thought of it,

---

[49] This quote from Mary Lyon left a deep impression on Rosetta when she was a young girl. See the August 30, 1891 diary.

Diary of Dr. Rosetta Hall 1892-1894

and it helps to make me content to do some things I don't like to do, and to leave undone many things I do like. And when another woman doctor or two can be found for Seoul, I think I shall be ready to go to the "Region beyond"[50] again, though it is always hard for me to pull up stakes and begin over. Somehow, I have a habit of getting things into a running order that is quite comfortable to myself and pleases others fairly well, and I am naturally just lazy enough to want to stay there; but thank God, some things, like the thoughts in the above quotation, stir me up to be willing, and to do things contrary to my naturally lazy self.

Tuesday, October 18—I am now expecting the arrival any moment of the Rev. and Mrs. Noble whom we have invited to live with us. I had a telegram from Fusan Saturday, saying they would arrive at Chemulpo Monday, and I learned the little steamboat would be up at 4 p.m. but something must have belated it for it is now 9:30 and I've only just received word that they'll be here soon. I am so sorry the Doctor is not here to help receive them—think they will be too. Doctor thinks a great deal of Mr. Noble; he helped Doctor in mission work in New York. Mr. Noble was then at Drew. He was ordained this summer, married just before to a pretty slight little creature of twenty I would say from the descriptions I've read of her. Oh, why don't they come? Have had the supper waiting so long, think it will not be very good.

---

[50] 2 Corinthians 10:16.

Diary of Dr. Rosetta Hall 1892-1894

10 p.m. They have come. Two such youngsters! I was prepared to find Mrs. Noble to look young, but I think Mr. Noble looks even younger. They are both very pleasant and nice I am sure. Mrs. Noble is from Wilkes-Barre[51] and called upon Dr. Stoeckel[52] before she came away. Mr. Noble is from Mount Rose[53], but doesn't know any of my relatives there.

I had the pleasure of giving them each their first mail after supper. Doctor had also written them a letter of greeting.

Wednesday, October 19—I can't imagine what has happened to my new gold pen during the night. I have been enjoying the use of it so much of late, and now all at once I find I can scarcely write with it. I expect "the boy" has been trying it. I am so disappointed, for steel pens rust and spoil so very quickly in this climate, and was just beginning to feel that I had something to rely upon, and now it is spoiled.

Doctor has been away four weeks today. Deary me, people do pester me so much, asking me when he expects to return. All I can answer is that he didn't say anything about returning.

Both Mr. and Mrs. Noble seem to be quite anxious to get it definitely settled as to the how they will live here, as

---

[51] Wilkes-Barre, Pennsylvania.
[52] Rosetta's medical college mate.
[53] Mount Rose, New Jersey.

each took occasion separately to speak to me about it already this forenoon.

They know quite well the Doctor's wish in the matter, that we have things in common and share the expenses so as to make it more economical for all; but as is quite natural to any newly married couple, as for that matter for anyone, they seem to prefer to keep house upon their own hook. They have been planning to do so it seems even if they had not more than two rooms and they thought they would keep no servants at all, and so be economical in that way. They have ordered their supplies (and these are at Chemulpo) with that plan in view. Rev. Appenzeller also advised them by all means to keep house by themselves. They however wish to do what is best in the matter, and finding that we were expecting them to live with us has a great weight with them especially as Mr. Noble knows and appreciates the Doctor so well, but I can see that they would both have to fight the same battle that I did before they could do it. Strange, but it seems to me that the Doctor did not have to do this. Is it pure selfishness with me and not them? We are all very anxious to do what is right, and what will render us able to save the most of help others to come to the field. But somehow, to me at least, it does seem unnatural for us to even think of trying to all live together in this way, but if it ever did to Doctor, he has kept it so well to himself that I can't think it even. I have tried to do the same, so far as I am concerned, with the Noble's. In fact, not knowing their minds at all, and expecting they would agree with the Doctor, I have been thinking for so long that it must be, that I have almost grown to like the

Diary of Dr. Rosetta Hall 1892-1894

idea, and shall be disappointed now if we can't carry it out. I tell them not to be in a hurry. There is plenty of time to decide the matter that they shall be my guests until the Doctor returns, and by that time they will know more of life in Korea and can better tell what they would like to do. I have had no occasion to speak of my own feelings in the matter, and would not do so anyhow. I hide myself behind the Doctor's wishes and say <u>we</u> when expressing them. Both Mr. and Mrs. Noble have lovely Christian characters, and I am sure we can get on with each other all right should we deem it best to undertake it. I do wish the Doctor were here, and yet I don't know but that it is more fair to the Nobles that he is not, for he has a faculty of persuading people do things quite against their wills often, and though as a rule, it is right and best, yet perhaps in this instance, it may not be? I do wonder how it will turn out. I think, however, it is more likely to go the Doctor's way than otherwise because it is almost 할수없소[54]. I think they will find it quite impossible to get along without at least one servant, and unless they do, there is pretty scant room. It could be managed, however.

All of our Mission people called here this forenoon. I had Rev. Jones in for tiffin, and we were all up to W. F. M. S. for dinner tonight. As we didn't get to bed until after 11 p.m. last night, I feel a bit tired and think I'll try and get there before 10 tonight.

---

[54] *Halsueupso,* Impossible or unbendable, an expression of resignation.

Diary of Dr. Rosetta Hall 1892-1894

Saturday, October 22, 10 p.m.—Just got back from an evening with Mrs. Greathouse and the General. There were some 12 or 15 people there. We were invited over to sing Gospel hymns, as a few times before the Doctor went away. Rev. Jones led in prayer at Mrs. Greathouse's request, as we came away. The General does seem to enjoy the songs so much. "Only an Armour Bearer"[55] particularly pleases him. Mrs. Greathouse likes "The Ninety and Nine"[56] and "Where is My Wandering Boy Tonight."[57] This evening Miss Heard, Colonel Nienstead[58] and Mr. Dombquey were present from outside the Mission circle.

I miss Doctor so much tonight. I had thought it possible he might come today. I received a letter yesterday from him written October 8th, but he said nothing about coming home then. He is quite well, studies every morning and treats patients in the afternoon. He had just gone down the Ta Tong River some 60 li to see the Captain of a small steamer that goes from Chemulpo to that place 3 or 4 times a year. He found that freight and a few passengers could go this way very reasonably; the trip is made in 29 hours or so. It would be quite an easy route for a lady to go to Pyong Yang. Doctor had not yet gotten either of my letters. Think he must have the last one by this time. If he stays much longer I shall be sorry I did not write again, but

---

[55] Words and music by Philip P. Bliss, 1838-1876).
[56] Words by Elizabeth C. Clephane (1830-1869), Musci by Ira David Sankey(1840-1908).
[57] Words and music by Robert Lowry (1826-1899).
[58] Col. F.J.H. Nienstead of the U.S. Consulate, Kobe, arrived in Korea 1888 and served as a military instructor for King Kojong's Army. He left Korea in 1898.

Diary of Dr. Rosetta Hall 1892-1894

I supposed he would be back before another would have a chance to reach him. Tomorrow, October 23rd, is Doctor's spiritual birthday, and he is down upon the schedule to preach that day. I wish it might have come so he could. I wonder if he is preparing, any sermons in the country, so far as I know, he didn't even take a Bible with him in English, carrying out very literally the Bishop's advice to stop all English reading. I do hope he is getting on nicely with the Korean, and I believe he is. It is his best chance. The moment he comes back, there will be so much work put upon him, I fear there will be but little time for study. I do pray that the Doctor may have a rich and glorious day tomorrow, that he may see many Koreans born into the Kingdom that this birthday may indeed be a blessed one to his soul, and I believe it will.

Diary of Dr. Rosetta Hall 1892-1894

Saturday Oct. 22

My dearest sister Mrs Hall

I hope you are well tonight. I think I will make you feel not very glad. After I came up my madame see me and she go tell Mrs Scranton about my story and she told her she do not like me go down hospital any more but I tell her I will help you this winter. Then she say yes you can help her this winter. I am afraid if I do not go hospital and help you then I will not see you any more. I am feel so bad because I cannot help you. Seem to me I part with you. I feel very bad now, but you trust that I will help you when I get marry. You must not think I do not help you any more I will help you sure. I wish you could see my heart

Letter from Esther Kim, page 1

Diary of Dr. Rosetta Hall 1892-1894

Letter from Esther Kim, page 2

Saturday, October 22

My dearest sister Mrs. Hall,

    I hope you are well tonight. I think I will make you feel not very glad. After I came up my Ma came see me and she go tell Mrs. Scranton about my story and she told her she do not like me go down hospital anymore. But I tell her I

Diary of Dr. Rosetta Hall 1892-1894

will help you this winter. Then she says yes you can help her this winter. I am afraid if I do not go hospital and help you then I will not see you anymore. I am feel so bad because I cannot help you. Seem to me I part with you. I feel very bad now, but you trust that I will help you when I get marry. You must not think I do not help you anymore. I will help you sure. I wish you could see my heart feel and how my heart jump and I cannot tell how much I feel bad for you. And I am sorry because I cannot help my dear sister, but I trust I will help you after I get marry. I hope you take me wherever you go. If you go 의주[Euiju] or 평안[Pyong An] take me. I will help. I will tell you some more next day.

From your dear sister,

Esther

Monday, November 7, 1892

And He said unto me, My grace is sufficient for thee: for my strength is made perfect in weakness. Most gladly therefore will I glory in my infirmities that the power of Christ may rest upon me. II Cor. 12:9 (Doctor's text yesterday afternoon at the Union Church.)

> "The heavier cross, the heartier prayer—
>   The bruised reeds most fragrant are;
> If wind and sky were always fair
>   The sailor would not watch the star;
> And David's Psalms had ne'er been sung
>   If grief his heart had never wrung."[59]

---

[59] "Je grösser Kreuz, je näher Himmel (Bearing the Cross)" from the German hymn writier Benjamin Schmolck(1672-1737)

Diary of Dr. Rosetta Hall 1892-1894

I hardly know what to write tonight. Since last I wrote in my journal, the Doctor has come, and has gone again. He was home twelve days, but they went by like a dream, and now the waiting time has come again. "This is but a life of waiting from the cradle to the grave."[60]

Oh, it was a so hard to think of his going for so long again, even much harder than before. Day by day our love grows stronger and separation makes our hearts ache. Before dawn Sunday morning, I had such a sense of my coming loneliness and longing for the homecoming again that for the first time I had to relieve a little of the heart-ache by crying. And all day Sunday, tears were bound to make their appearance about my strongest efforts to banish them; and I began to fear after the Doctor had gone no one could speak to me of him without my making a baby of myself. But now the day has passed and I have not shed a single tear, and I feel quite brave tonight. Surely God's grace is sufficient.

I used to have but a faint idea of what it meant for husband and wife to part for a length of time; but now I can appreciate well some little dialogues that Doctor showed me in the life of Livingstone. Here is a quotation:

"Oh David! David! You can't tell what I have suffered while waiting for you. Do not let us apart again. ++ I must go back with you, if you return to Africa."

"Yes, and you shall, Mary. The separation has been very bitter for me too; but I felt I was in the path of duty, and

---

[60] From the poem "Waiting" by H. E. Randall.

Diary of Dr. Rosetta Hall 1892-1894

though it was like tearing my heart from my body, I felt I dared not refuse to go forward at the call of God."

Letters from Korean students and helpers to Rosetta:

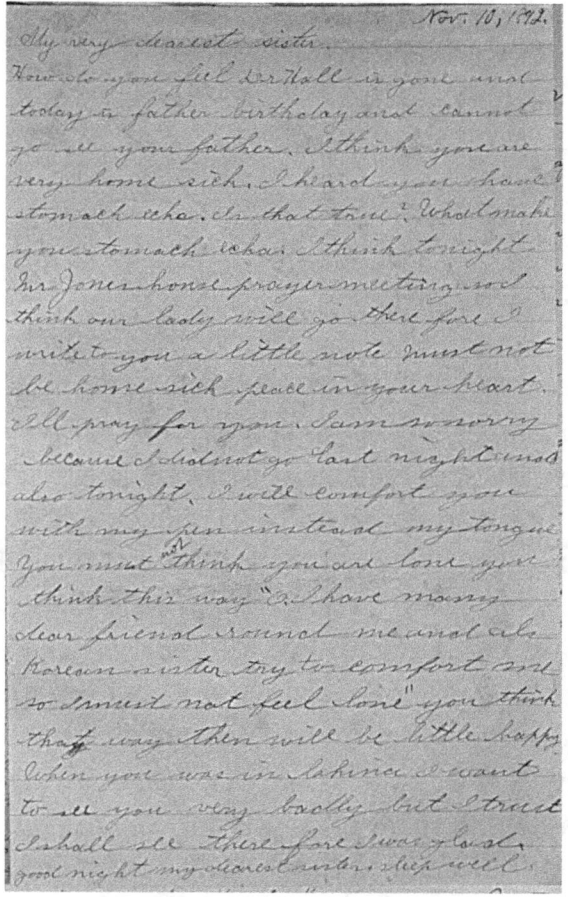

Unsigned letter, likely from Esther Kim

Diary of Dr. Rosetta Hall 1892-1894

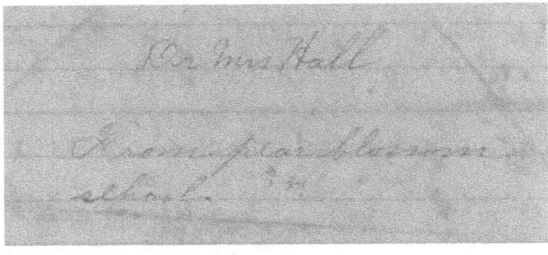

From Pear Blossom School[61]

November 10, 1892

My very dearest sister,

How do you feel? Dr. Hall is gone and today is father birthday and cannot go see your father. I think you are very homesick. I heard you have stomachache. Is that true? What make you stomachache? I think tonight Mr. Jones house prayer meeting so I think our lady will go therefore I write to you a little note. Must not be homesick place in your heart. I will pray for you. I am sorry because I did not go last night and also tonight. I will comfort you with my pen instead my tongue. You must not think you are lone. You think this way. "O, I have many dear friend round me and also Korean sister try to comfort me so I must not feel lone." You think that way then will be little happy. When you were in China, I want to see you very badly but I trust I shall see therefore I was glad. Good night my dear sister, sleep well.

---

[61] Ewha Girls' School.

Diary of Dr. Rosetta Hall 1892-1894

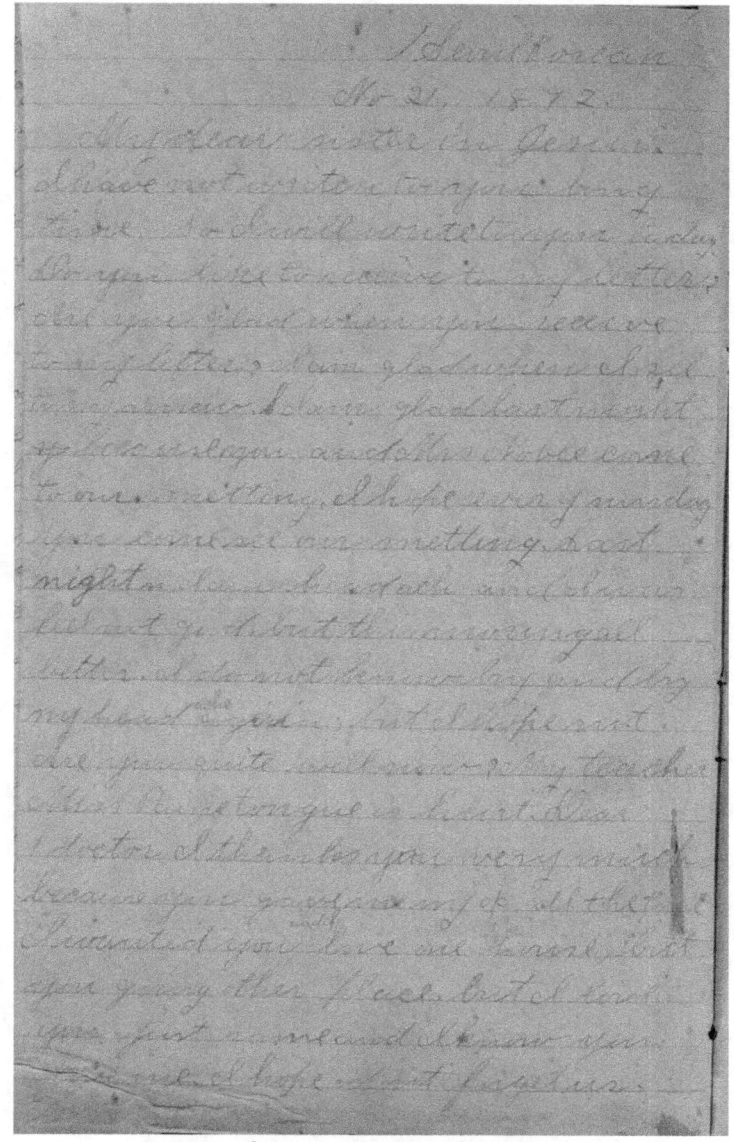

Letter from Annie Cassidy, page 1

Diary of Dr. Rosetta Hall 1892-1894

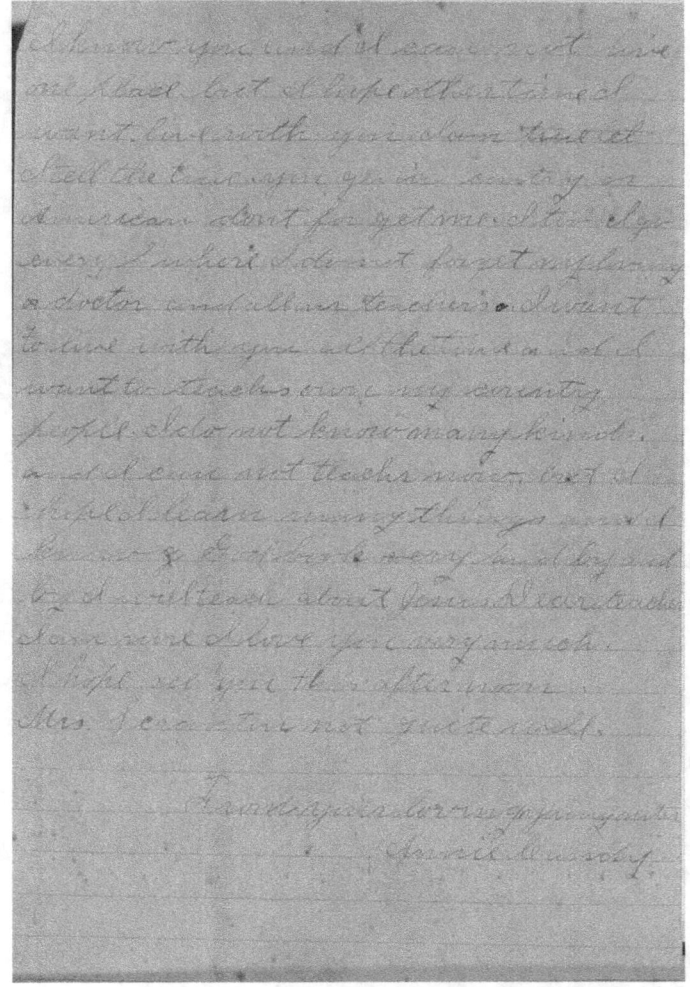

Letter from Annie Cassidy, page 2

Seoul, Korea
November 21, 1892

My dear sister in Jesus,

I have not written you long time. So I will write to your to-

Diary of Dr. Rosetta Hall 1892-1894

day. Do you like to receive to my letter? Are you glad when you receive to my letter? I am glad when I see to my answer. I am glad last night because you and Mrs. Noble came to our meeting. I hope every Sunday you come see our meeting. Last night I am headache and I was feel not good, but this morning all better. I do not know by and by my headache again, but I hope not. Are you quite well now? My teacher Miss Paine tonight is hurt. Dear doctor I thank you very much because you gave me my 약[yak][62] and the time. I wanted you and I live one house but you going other place. But I love you just same and I know you love me. I hope don't forget us. I know you and I cannot live one place, but I hope other time I want live with you. I tell the true. You go in country or America don't forget me. I too I go everywhere I do not forget my loving doctor and all our teachers. I want to live with you all the time and I want to teach own my country people. I do not know many kinds and I cannot teach now, but I hope I learn many things and I know God book and by and by I will teach about Jesus. Dear teacher I am sure I love you very much. I hope see you this afternoon. Mrs. Scranton not quite well.

From your loving young sister,

Annie Cassidy

---

[62] Medicine.

Diary of Dr. Rosetta Hall 1892-1894

My very dearest sister

I hope you are very happy in your heart. I wish I could go every night and talk to you and comfort you. I am so sorry my dearest sister feel so bad and stay lonely. I am fear you get sick. Monday you was so unhappy and you look so sober. Now I think you think of him very much. Monday night I was with you therefore you laugh so well. But tonight you feel so sad. I think my very dearest sister must not feel so bad. God will help your dear husband. Don't be trouble in your heart. You feel so sad because your dear husband go so. Don't when you told me you will get marry but now not feel bad as much as before, so you will you feel so bad now. I am very glad you love him so much. Just now I thought many things now I know why lady love gentle man how much good your dear doctor stay with you all the time. I hope my brother dr Hall help well. How can live on Korean food. I am afraid to get sick. I think you don't believe are sure way for dr Hall

Unsigned letter, likely from Esther Kim, page 1

but it's true I do not feel so bad as much as you do but I have some trouble. I hope be strong and health, the good health is God best gift to us. Well I want to comfort you but I cannot, tonight Susan been her home to see her mother I rather go my dearest sister house I want go my dear mother's home but I cannot go because I am afraid Chinese men. now I must close my dear sister. From your darling sister.

To my dear doctor Mrs Hall

Unsigned letter, likely from Esther Kim, page 2

Diary of Dr. Rosetta Hall 1892-1894

My very dearest sister,

I hope you are very happy in your heart. I wish I could go every night and talk to you and comfort you. I am so sorry my dearest sister feels so bad and stay lonely. I am fear you get sick. Monday you was so unhappy and you look so somber now. I think you think of him very much. Monday night I was with you therefore you laugh some but tonight you feel so sad I think my very admire sister must not feel so bad. God will help your dear husband. Do not be trouble in your heart. You feel so sad because your dear husband go so do I. When you told me you will get marry, but now not feel bad as much as before so you see you feel so bad now. I am very glad you love him so much. Just now I thought many things. Now I know why lady love gentleman. How much good your dear doctor stay with you all the time. I hope my brother Dr. Hall keep well. How can he live on Korean food? I am afraid he get sick. I think you do not believe me. I am sorry for Dr. Hall but it's true I do not feel so bad as much as you do but I have some trouble. I hope he strong and health. The good health is God but gifts to us. Well I want to comfort you but I cannot. Tonight Susan been her home to see her mother. I rather go my dearest sister house I want go my dear mother's home. But I cannot go because I am afraid Chinese man. Now I must close my dear sister.

From your darling sister,

[Unsigned, likely Esther Kim]

Diary of Dr. Rosetta Hall 1892-1894

> Seoul Korea
> Nov 23. 18. 92.
>
> My dear teacher Mrs Hall. I do not write to you long time, I think tomorrow is thankgiving, so I write few words to comfort you. I am sorry because your dear loving husband is not with you on thankgiving day. I hope you have good time tomorrow Are you quite well. We all very well but our loving Mrs Scranton has sick. I want Mrs Scranton better soon. When she sick we all feel very sorry. I think God will help her and bless her also. I hope you feel happy and have peaceful in you heart If I know speak English well then I will say many loving words to you just like other girl and write to you letter and show my love. I love you just much as other grils

Letter from Susanna, page 1

Diary of Dr. Rosetta Hall 1892-1894

Letter from Susanna, page 2

great deal. but you must
not feel comfort you. I think
your dear husband think of
you great deal, and he want to
see you and he will be home
sick to but do for Jesus so you
must not feel so bad. next
time I will write to you
some time but now I must
close. I hope you answer my
letter Good night dear Mrs.
Hall.

From your loving friend

Miss Susanna

Letter from Susanna, page 3

Diary of Dr. Rosetta Hall 1892-1894

Seoul Korea
November 23, 1892

My dear teacher Mrs. Hall,

I do not write to you long time. I think tomorrow is Thanksgiving so I write few words to comfort you. I am sorry because your dear loving husband is not with you on Thanksgiving Day. I hope you have good time tomorrow. Are you quite well? We all very well but our loving Mrs. Scranton has sick. I want Mrs. Scranton better soon. When she sick we all feel very sorry. I think God will help her and bless her also. I hope you feel happy and have peaceful in your heart. If I know speak English well then I will say many loving words to you just like other girl and write to you letter and show my love. I love you just much as other girls but I do not show very much. Therefore people think I am unmerciful girl but I have loving heart. You think I am unmerciful girl? I think you have no letter for me. If you do not like answer my letter but you ought answer my letter even you do not like. I know you will answer my letter. If you time but only I speak that way. I hope our bless Jesus bless you and keep you near His loving side and help you and make you happy all your lifetime. Please excuse my poor sentence and writing. I think you will be homesick because your dear husband is gone and you feel quite lone. I think your father and your mother and brother and sister and friends will think of you great deal. But you must not feel comfort you. I think your dear husband think of you great deal, and he want to see you and he will be homesick to but do for Jesus so you must not feel so bad. Next time I will write to you sometime now I must close. I hope answer my letter. Good night dear Mrs. Hall.

From your loving friend,
Miss Susanna

Diary of Dr. Rosetta Hall 1892-1894

Thanksgiving day

My very dearest sister. How are you this morning? I am very sorry for you because your dear doctor went to country and leave you lone. I think your dear father and mother and brother and sister think of you very much. You must not be homesick. I think you more feel unhappy because your dear doctor is gone but you trust me I will comfort you. My very dearest sister I write to you to many time therefore you get tired of my letter but I will write to you again today. I hope you are very happy today and keep well. This time I feel so sad again. Last year you live with me and say many sweet things to me but this year you and part away not stay each, it make me feel so sad in my heart. Christmas time is soon make me glad one side but other side make me feel sad. This time I feel so humble, and do much work for Him. I want you feel happy with me and work

Unsigned letter likely from Esther Kim, page 1

Diary of Dr. Rosetta Hall 1892-1894

Unsigned letter likely from Esther Kim, page 2 and 3

Diary of Dr. Rosetta Hall 1892-1894

Thanksgiving Day

To My dear sister Mrs. Hall

My very dearest sister,

How are you this morning? I am very sorry for you because your dear doctor went to country and leave you lone. I think your dear father and mother and brother and sister think of you very much. You must not be homesick. I think you more feel unhappy because your dear doctor is gone. But you trust me I will come for you. My very dearest sister, I write to you too many time therefore you get tired of my letter but I will write to you again today. I hope you are very happy today and keep well. This time I feel so sad again. Last year you live with me and say many sweet things to me but this year you and [I] part away and not stay each, it make me feel so sad in my heart. Christmas time is soon make me glad one side, but other side to make me feel sad. This time I feel so humble and do much work for Him. I want you feel happy with me and work for Jesus in place. I hope God make every people of Korea all believe in Him and love. God has wonderful power. He can make that away if He want. I heard great many things make me feel bad but I pray to God give me wide heart and I do not believe them but I know you love me and I know I love you. I wish I could go now and comfort you and happy each other. Now I do not care. You show my letter to girls. You did not stay with me therefore I do not fear anymore. I will leave this house very soon. They will leave school before I leave. I am very glad our dear Mrs. Scranton invite you this afternoon. You will go Mrs. Bunker tonight eat supper? I

Diary of Dr. Rosetta Hall 1892-1894

think every people are good to you. I am so sorry for Mrs. Scranton. I never write to you on Thanksgiving day but this I write you a few words. I think your dear doctor will think about you. I am very glad because he went country and teach people of 평양 [Pyong Yang]. I hope you will be happy today. I'll pray for you. Love to Mr. and Mrs. Noble. I want write to her but I cannot. I have time to write to you but I have no time to write to other lady who my friend because when I write to you anything that come from heart and I write. To other lady I try make sentence right and make sound good therefore I have it all time. Good by my very sweet sister.

From your faithful sister,

[Unsigned, likely Esther Kim]

Monday, December 5, 1892

What shall I say? He hath spoken unto me, and Himself hath done it. Isa. 38:15

> "Himself hath done it."— He who searched me through
> Sees how I cling to earth's ensnaring ties;
> And so he breaks each reed on which my soul
> Too much for happiness and joy relies.
> "Himself hath done it" all! Oh, how those words
> Should hush to silence every murmuring thought!

Diary of Dr. Rosetta Hall 1892-1894

> "Himself hath done it!" — He who loves me best, —
> He who my soul with his own blood hath bought.[63]

I find the above in *Between the Lights: Thoughts for the Quiet Hour* for today—a book that Dr. and Mrs. Dowkoutt[64] gave Doctor. I often find in it just what I like for the day, and I enjoy it, and "Crumbs from the King's Table" that Mrs. Skidmore gave me very much.

This has been quite a busy day. It didn't begin very early with me because the stove pipe had become so choked up with soot from that troublesome Japanese coal, the boy could not get the fire started, until after he took the pipe down and cleaned it out, and that means everything and everybody in the room covered with anything but snowflakes. I got out as soon as I could, and despairing of having breakfast in my room for the morning, had it brought into Mrs. Noble's room, but it was 9 o'clock before we got through with breakfast and prayers.

For economy's sake, that we may be more certain of fulfilling our promise of becoming responsible for one-half the salary of another doctor to Korea for 2 years, we have abolished the both dining room and bedroom for the winter, and have these together with sitting room and study all in one room. It goes very nicely. Doctor fixed the bed to turn up against the wall inunder a shelf from which hangs

---

[63] From "Himself hath done it" by C. Fawcett.
[64] Dr. George D. Dowkoutt.

a curtain, so it doesn't show for the day, and he made a light dining table, that is just set into the room before meals and taken out after. Rev. and Mrs. Noble did conclude to live with us, and this month Mrs. Noble is taking her turn at housekeeping for the first. We are getting along very nicely, and I'm sure are as happy as anyone could be under similar circumstances and I think a bit more so.

This afternoon I taught my class in Physiology. Have just finished "circulation" with them. Saw to having some cloth measured out for our boy another suit of clothes, then went to the dispensary and treated twenty-five patients, and went out to visit a sick women of the 량반[yangban]class over half-hour chair ride from here, didn't get home till 6:30. Mrs. Noble had been to a birthday party of Willa Ohlinger's[65] so was not in any hurry for supper, having had lots of nice cake there.

My dear husband has been gone one whole month today, and not one word from him yet. When he was in America I heard from him oftener than this. I am glad Mr. Lee[66] is with him for if anything was the matter we would be more sure to hear.

9:30 p.m. A letter has just come from the Doctor, and though in one place he speaks of not returning till Christmas as he expected when he went away at a later date he writes that he might leave in a week's time, if Mr. Lee was well enough to start. It seems he has been very sick. So

---

[65] Willa Ohlinger (1884-1893) died in May 1893, after her brother Bertie died.
[66] Rev. Graham Lee of Presbyterian Mission.

they may be home any time now as this letter was nearly two weeks in coming.

Doctor feels that the way is opening up in a wonderful way for his work in Pyong Yang. Soon after he reached the city, he went to visit a little boy who was his patient there before, and had quite recovered. His father is a man of means with a position with the Governor, and he was so delighted to see the doctor again, and invited him to make his home there, gave him and Mr. Lee the two best rooms in the house, and said he was more glad to see him than he would be to see his parents. It is a large 35 *kang* house on a hill with a beautiful yard in front and to one side, though it is right in the midst of the city and in a good place for dispensary and evangelistic work. Later Doctor asked the man if he knew where he could purchase a similar property, and the next evening he offered to sell his own house to him for $780, and that is Doctor's object in returning to get permission to purchase the same and to raise money for it.[67]

Doctor does hope our work will be together next year. Separation is such a trial but he says we don't want to sacrifice the Master's work to please ourselves and writes, "I am glad after all, my darling that God permits us to do hard things for Him. It is a special mark of favor, let us not worry but be brave for Jesus sake and get all the blessing from this trial that it is His will to bestow. God is training us and

---

[67] See William James Hall's mission letter written on December 21, 1892 (Appendix 2). The price of the 35-kan house was 780 yen.

Diary of Dr. Rosetta Hall 1892-1894

getting us ready for lives of greater usefulness and it is all right. "

11 p.m. I was a bit late getting to bed tonight, and just before I was ready who should walk in but the dear Doctor! How happy we both are tonight. Separation is so hard but the joy of meeting again is very great.

Letter from Esther Kim, Christmas 1892

To: 의원부인 [Doctor *Puene*[68]]

My very dear friend doctor,

Tomorrow is Christmas day. Therefore I give you three thimbles. I love you very much therefore I give you this thimble. This is not pretty but please take with my love.

From your truly truly friend,

Esther

---

[68] *Puene* is equivalent to Madame, a respectful title for a married woman.

Diary of Dr. Rosetta Hall 1892-1894

Letter from Esther Kim, February 20, 1893, page 1

Diary of Dr. Rosetta Hall 1892-1894

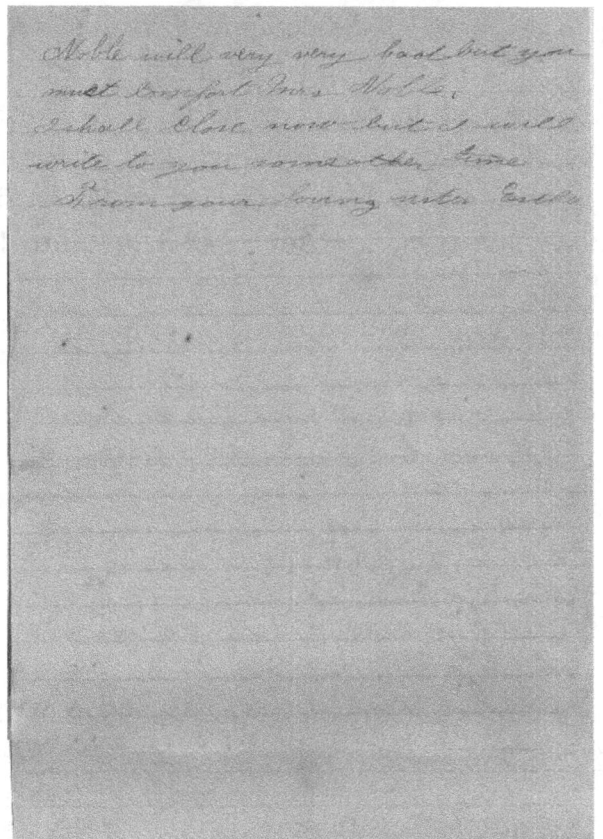

Letter from Esther Kim, February 20, 1893, page 2

Monday morning, February 20, 1893

My very sweet dearest darling sister,

How are you today? Are you feel very bad? My darling sister I know how you feel. I know you feel so lonesome; but my darling sister remember how much I love and must not feel so lonesome. I am so sorry for you but Lord want the work up in 평양 [Pyong Yang] so we cannot help. I know how you feel because I was feel so sad and unhappy be-

Diary of Dr. Rosetta Hall 1892-1894

cause you get married and go China. Just think of that you know how much I love. So you feel bad because dear Dr. Hall go country but he will come back and live with you all your life but I do not know I will live with you or not. But I do not feel bad any more so you must not feel bad. I want to comfort you very much. Don't feel bad. I think Mrs. Noble will very very bad but you must comfort Mrs. Noble. I shall close now but I will write to you some other time.

From your loving sister,

Esther

Monday, March 28, 1893

Be ye therefore followers of God, as dear children, and <u>walk in love</u>. Eph. v. 1,2

> "As unto the bow the cord is,
> So unto the man is woman,
> Though she bends him, she obeys him,
> Though she draws him, yet she follows,
> Useless each without the other!"
> —From *The Song of Hiawatha*[69]

I have just returned from the Great East Gate, where I began medical work[70] the 15th of this month, going there

---

[69] By Henry Wadsworth Longfellow (1807–1882).
[70] The East Gate or Aogi Dispensary work was started in 1889 but with return of Dr. Meta Howard, the work had been closed in 1890. Rosetta opened the new work at the East Gate on March 15, 1893. The Story of

Diary of Dr. Rosetta Hall 1892-1894

every Tuesday and Friday. I do not have much work there yet, as the people have scarcely found it out, and the carpenters are still working at the buildings, but we have a nice site for work there, and I am sure it will grow. I had 7 patients at the dispensary, and one out-call today. Yesterday I had 31 dispensary patients here, and 8 in-patients. Have had some interesting cases lately. Did an operation for scirrhus[71] of the breast, removing the whole breast and cleaning out the axilla. That is doing well. Have an uterine fibroid now that I think I may operate upon. Have had some cases in ascites and general anasarca that have been surprising. One poor woman who had not walked since last September and who was swollen up tight all over came walking in the dispensary to bid me "goodbye" yesterday. And a boy of ten who was in rather worse condition, if anything, is so much better after three days treatment, that his mother would like to take him home today.

We have very interesting religious instruction in the waiting room each day before I see the patient conducted by Miss Lewis and Mary Hoang.

Doctor has been gone five weeks today, and on his fourth trip to Pyong Yang and his second to We Chu.[72] It is just 9 months ago today we were married. They have been months full of happiness, and yet they have had their own trials.

---

the Woman's Foreign Missionary Society of the Methodist Episcopal Church 1869 – 1895, p169-174.
[71] A cancerous tumor.
[72] See Letter to Dr. Leonard written by William James Hall regarding this trip (Appendix 5).

Diary of Dr. Rosetta Hall 1892-1894

"And e'en as prudent parents disallow
Too much sweet to craving baby food"

So God has seen fit to discipline us by these weeks of separation and by not giving us a home of our own and to ourselves. Also we have wounded each other's feelings by words. Once I was most at fault, and another time the Doctor, but not a half hour went by in either case before we asked and received full pardon from each other and from our Heavenly Father. And though at the time we regretted a thousand times that such a trouble ever happened, yet now "looking backward,"[73] I believe God has even made that work for our good. It has shown us points we need to strengthen by God's help; and the depth of our love for each other has been measured in another way, a painful one to be sure, but nonetheless true, and I know we love each other today more than we ever did. I want to quote from Doctor's last letter dated March 16th.

> "Your precious letter reached me on Tuesday, although it was as long as I could expect, yet while I was reading it I was dreading that each page would be the last. Tonight my whole soul goes out to you in love, I have in you, my dear, the desire of my heart. I praise God more and more each day for giving me such a precious treasure. You are my perfect ideal. I could not ask for more in my wife than I have in you my darling."

Another time he writes,

---

[73] This quotation is likely from the book *Looking Backward* by Edward Bellamy. See September 18, 1890 diary.

Diary of Dr. Rosetta Hall 1892-1894

> "My whole being yearns for you. It is in times like this that I realize how dearly I love you and how much you are to me, but we will cheerfully give up all for Jesus."

So all that has happened to us has but bound us the closer in heart, and the bitter is by far out balanced by the sweet. God is so good to us. How can I ever praise him as I ought for giving me my husband. "We love, because He first loved us."[74] "Love so amazing so divine, demands my life, my love, my all."[75]

Doctor writes me that he has been able to purchase two very desirable pieces of property[76]—one near the West Gate on the main road to be Clinic, which will be just the place for Medical and Evangelistic work, and another farther back and higher up where it would be nice for us to live. He is hoping I may return with him in May when he comes back this time, and I want to very much. We are expecting our new lady Dr. Cutler[77] this week, so probably I can be spared for a month or two. Doctor was having from 50 to 60 patients per day, and the work has so grown in favor the Governor who hitherto has been difficult to deal

---

[74] 1 John 4:19.
[75] From "When I Survey the Wondrous Cross" by Isaac Watts (1674-1748).
[76] See the letter written by William James Hall to Rev. Henry Appenzeller around this time (Appendix 3).
[77] Dr. Mary M. Cutler (1865-1948) graduated from the University of Michigan Medical School and served as a medical missionary in Korea from 1892 to 1933. She worked with Rosetta at PoKuNoKwan, Ewha Girls' School, and Pyong Yang Extended Grace Women's Hospital, retired in 1933, and returned to America in 1939.

Diary of Dr. Rosetta Hall 1892-1894

with, replied to some who went to him to ask him to remove them.

> "The foreigner is not a bad man, but a gentleman. He who cares the sick and helps the poor, is he not a good man? The same work is going on in Seoul, and you need not be afraid of him."

And he issued a proclamation stating this, and that these foreigners had permission from the King to travel in the interior, and anyone who interfered or made trouble with him, must be brought before the Governor. So Doctor thinks that already as much has been accomplished to remove prejudice as 3 years of ordinary work. Reverends Moffett, Lee and Swallen of the Presbyterian Church have gone up there now. They had not bought yet, but were going to move in Doctor's house when he and Rev. Noble went on to We Chu for which they expected to start March 20th. They are working there now I suppose, and next Monday will start back for Seoul, reaching here about April 15th.

God surely is wonderfully opening up the way for work in the North Interior, and I long to begin work for women there. When I asked Esther if she would be willing to go to Pyong Yang to work for Jesus she replied,

> "I will go wherever Lord open door for me, if He open door in Pyong Yang I will go. I give my body and soul and heart to the Lord. My body and my heart and my soul are all the Lord's things, and I give up my life to teach my people about God even if people kill me. I do not hope I get rich or have many

pretty things, but I want to work for Jesus most of all."

It is truly marvelous the way in which that girl has grown spiritually for the last year. She didn't used to like to sew, and always managed to get someone else to do it for her, but now she works away faithfully at it. I have gotten Miss Bengel to teach her to play on the organ, naturally she has not the patience to practice, but she <u>does</u> it and is learning so well. She controls her temper so much better, and scarcely ever does a wrong act now. She studies her Bible, and surely the Holy Spirit is her teacher; she understands and can explain it to others so well. She is very discerning and wise in her ways. She cannot have an easy time of it, for the others, even to Mrs. Yi, are jealous of her superior powers, but she is not proud, and tries in every way not to make others feel uncomfortable. The letter of February 20 that I have placed in before writing this day shows how she enters into and appreciates my present trial. I must quote her own words from a letter written just before the Korean New Year, which will show another change in Esther.

> "I am very glad because Dr. Hall gather all his money, I am not glad because he will left you lone, but I am very very glad because he go up Pyong Yang and teach about God and bring them to our blessed Jesus and make them good and kind therefore I am glad. I think about Dr. Hall going 평안도 [Pyong An Province]. I pray for him every day when I study Bible. Did you hear when I pray for man? I tell you how my heart get different. Before I do not love Dr. Hall and always I do not like Dr. Hall come see you,

but this time I do love him and I would like to see him. That is one way my heart different and something else, before I feel so bad because you get marry, but now I have no trouble, and I have peace in my heart. I am glad because you get married and have happy heart."

Such a depth of character as Esther has, none but those who know her well would think it though, as her personal appearance and manners, unfortunately, would never suggest it to a stranger. However, she is improving in these respects also, is going much more intelligent looking, and womanly in manners. Sometimes she looks really beautiful to me.

> "It gives to beauty half its power
> The matchless charm worth all the rest,
> The light that dances o'er the face
> And speaks of sunshine in the breast,
> If beauty ne'er have set her seal
> It well supplies her absence too,
> And any cheek looks passing fair
> Whene'er a sunny heart shines through."[78]

I am not getting much time to study Korean, when I think of it, it is really discouraging, and it seems as if I would never know the language. My medical duties take up at least half of each day, sometimes more, and then though I don't spend much time with household duties, yet there is a portion of time put in that necessary work. As this morning I had to make arrangements for coolies to make coal balls of our coal dust, as suddenly we find ourselves

---

[78] From "The Merry Heart" by John Greenleaf Whittier.

Diary of Dr. Rosetta Hall 1892-1894

out of fuel to burn, then I bought 20 pounds of beef, and put it down for "corn beef" according to a receipt[79] father used at home; and then I looked at the cucumbers we laid down last fall, and I found them very nice, so took out a lot to freshen for pickles. Then Mrs. Noble had mentioned how fond she was of "Suet Pudding," and as I had some nice pieces of suet that I cut off of the beef I thought I'd look up a receipt and teach cook how to make one for to-morrow, and so this morning was spent.

In the afternoon I saw twenty-five patients at the dispensary, and then went to Ladies prayer meeting and Mrs. Junkin's[80]. This evening I had four Korean women, Mrs. Yi and Rachel, Mary Hoang and Susan here for supper, and as they couldn't be seen by men I waited on the table myself. We had a real nice visit with them. They staid till 9:30 p.m. and enjoyed themselves very much. Once before, we had a Korean party for supper, our cook's wife, mother, and sister, and Esther and Susanna. And several times we have had Korean women like Po-pe's grandmother or another woman's house where we visit often sit down and eat tiffin with us when they happened to be here at that time. Both Mrs. Noble and I enjoy it very much, as it seems to give them a great deal of pleasure, and they have so little in their lives.

---

[79] Recipe in archaic word. Today, the words "receipt" and "recipe" have clear separate meanings; however, both words are derived from the Latin word "recipere," which means "to take" or "to receive." When Chaucer first used "receipt" in *The Canterbury Tales* and when Lanfranc of Milan first used "recipe" in *Lanfranc's Cirurg*, both words were used for the medicinal prescriptions and preparations.
[80] Rev. and Mrs. William M. Junkin of the Southern Presbyterian Mission.

Diary of Dr. Rosetta Hall 1892-1894

This one woman, I think her name is Kim, she has been at the hospital, and Miss Lewis and I visited her house quite regularly through the winter once a week, has learned the whole catechism, and several songs from the Korean hymnbook. And the last time I was there I gave her the Apostle's Creed, and I have no doubt she will know it the next time we go. She seems just hungering and thirsting after righteousness. Po-pe has learned the Lord's Prayer, Happy Land, Just as I am Without One Plea, and Praise God From Whom All Blessings Flow, and has taught them to her little five-year-old brother. It is real cunning to hear him try to sing them. The baby there has been very sick this week, and I got the mother to bring it in the hospital for a few days so I could watch him better, and Po-pe came too. The father was also there a few times, the first I have seen him. The baby seems to be slowly growing better now, though I fear it is a tubercular child. In these two families, there are five who wish to be baptized, and whom we think might well be, so we feel that the Lord has blessed our efforts in this direction through the winter. This is such an affectionate and appreciative people. It is certainly a privilege and a pleasure to work among them, and I hope the Lord will grant us a long life here to be spent in His service.
[81]

"If I can only place one little brick in the pavement of the Lord's pathway, I will place it there, that com-

---

[81] For this family's story, see Rosetta's mission letter written on December 12, 1892 (Appendix 1).

ing generations may walk thereon to the Heavenly City." —Phillips Brooks[82]

Our last mail brought us news of the death of Phillips Brooks, also of Hayes[83] and Blaine[84]. I have had good news from home all winter, except in Annie's last letter she wrote some things that made me cry. She wrote that Mother was getting quite deaf, and that she had grown so old since I saw her, and that Father said, after they read the letter I wrote for his last birthday, he would like to live until I come home again and then he didn't care how soon he went. They are all quite well and strong I think. Father and Mother drove down to White Lake visiting this winter, so I think they must both be real smart, and I do trust that God will spare them both many years yet. It seems as if I <u>must</u> see them again. In Mother's last letter she says, "We are beginning to borrow trouble about you. Fear if you go to Pyong Yang, we won't hear from you so often. It's so nice to get a letter twice and sometimes three times a month. I have to thank God every time we hear from you. O, praise His name for His goodness toward us." Amen.

Joe sent me this message: "Take good care of yourself and don't get careless. I see your picture twice every day, and hope we will live to see each other again." And mother

---

[82] Phillips Brooks (1835 – January 17, 1893) was an American Episcopal clergyman and author, the Bishop of Massachusetts, particularly remembered as writer of the Christmas hymn, "O Little Town of Bethlehem".
[83] Rutherford B. Hayes (1822 – January 17, 1893), the 19th President of the Unites States.
[84] James G. Blaine (1830 – January 27, 1893), the 28th and 31st Unites States Secretary of State.

Diary of Dr. Rosetta Hall 1892-1894

adds, "I think this is the desire of his heart." Dear old black Joe, he always loved me so much from a little baby when he used to hold me on his knee and give me the bottle, and when I grew big enough to enjoy a ride with him in his buggy, and could appreciate candies and nuts, and Christmas and New Year's presents, on up to my beginning to teach school[85] when he let me have my first watch, and when I first went off to Oswego to school[86], he accompanied me on the journey, and whenever I have been away from home long, he has seen to it that they sent me a box of fruit, etc., and I could always expect to find some candies from Joe. He cannot write, or else no doubt I should hear from him often, but he sends me the Liberty Register every week for his letter, he says. Oh, I have so many loving friends, and so much real love is lavished upon me. "What shall I render unto the Lord for all his benefits toward me. ++ I will offer to Thee the sacrifice of Thanksgiving, and will call upon the name of the Lord." Psa. cxvi

Saturday, April 29, 1893

Guide our feet into the way of peace. Luke i. 79

"Which is the true, safe way —
Which would be vain?
I am not wise to know

---

[85] Rosetta obtained a Second Grade Teacher's Certificate at age 16 in October 1881 and started teaching at the Huntington District School on May 1, 1892. See Rosetta's timeline.
[86] After 3 months of teaching at the Huntington District School, Rosetta entered Oswego State Normal School on September 6, 1882.

Nor sure of foot to go;
My blind eyes cannot see
What is clear to Thee;
Lord, make it clear to me."[87]

Such a happy two weeks as the last have been. Doctor came home April 13th, two days before I expected him, and yet I thought of then possibility of his coming, and went and unlocked the door before I went to bed that night, and sure enough about 11 p.m. he came having traveled 140 li or 47 miles since morning. He is so glad to be home once more, and we are so happy together. He says he is just beginning to court me now, and though I thought he did very well before we were married, and during our first "honeymoon," I must confess he far surpasses both now. He seems to fall deeper and deeper in love each day; he just can't call me enough sweet names, or tell me how much he loves and appreciates me; and though I am sure he kisses me more than 100 times a day, and holds me in his arms and upon his knees, yet he can't seem to get close enough to me, he just wants to put me right into his big heart and carry me with him every moment. My! But I am silly, but just to think to have such a lover for a husband—it is so lovely it makes me feel like a girl of sweet sixteen instead of a matron of twenty-seven with a lot of gray hairs among the brown. Well, I never thought I could love any man like I do my dear husband, but he is such a good teacher—how can I help it? He says I teach him, that he was fast growing into a narrow old bachelor, but that now

---

[87] From "My Prayer" by an anonymous author.

his heart has widened, and his mind has broadened, so that he is sure he can do far better work in the world. I know I am a better woman.

But this is not what I started out to write when I selected my text and quotation for the day. I was going to write how that after Doctor had worked nearly over a month at Pyong Yang, and was gaining great favor among the people, he went with Mr. Noble to We Chu, and invited Reverends Moffett, Lee and Swallen who had come to Pyong Yang in the meantime to live in one of his houses until they could buy for themselves. After Doctor and Mr. Noble left Pyong Yang, the Presbyterian brothers succeeded in purchasing property outside of the city, but they had not much more than done so before the people became alarmed at so many foreigners purchasing property, though of course it had always been done in the name of their Korean helpers as according to treaty foreigners have no right to hold property outside of treaty ports. The Governor knew very well of Dr. Hall's relation to the purchase, and his plans for medical work there, and because they wanted the Doctor, he winked at it, and gave him his protection, but when so many more who were not doctors came in, he evidently changed his mind, at least he ordered Moffett to keep back his deeds to the former owner, and them to give the money back. And also the people made it so hot for Moffett and Lee, that they had to leave the city—Swallen had already left upon an Evangelistic tour through Whang Hae Do. The former owners of Doctor's houses moved back, but as Doctor had the deeds with him at We Chu, he is still the owner in the name of Mr. You, his interpreter. When he came back

Diary of Dr. Rosetta Hall 1892-1894

he was kindly received, and since he has been home he has received letters from both of the former owners telling him not to be anxious they will take good care of the property, and asking him to come back soon, that there are many sick people waiting for him.

At this same time, we are having slightly serious times in Söul. A politico-religious faction from the South called "Tong Hak" came to the Palace and petitioned the King to send all foreigners to their own country. The King paid but little attention to them except to order them back. They went saying they'd return last Saturday, 40,000 strong and they'd kill [all] of the foreigners themselves. Some felt a great deal of anxiety as the day approached, especially the Japanese. The King sent guards to all of our compounds, by day they were disguised as farmers but at night they were soldiers with musket and bayonet. They are still on guard, but everything has remained quiet. For a time, it made a difference in the attendance of dispensary patients, especially at the East Gate. The people feared if they were seen going in and out of the foreigner's house, they too would be killed; but I think it is blowing over now, for day before yesterday, I had 27 patients here, and yesterday had 13 at the East Gate. However, all things together it hardly seems expedient for me to return with Doctor to Pyong Yang, as we have both been so much in hopes that I could do. I am very much disappointed and can scarcely give it up yet. I did so much want to see how they would receive me there before the Annual Meeting, so that if possible we could make arrangements to move there soon after. But now Doctor thinks it the better policy to make policy slowly,

//
and he will go back with Mr. You alone, and he feels sure he can get things in good shape again, and then as it will probably be impossible for me to go with him next fall, he hopes that another year Dr. Busteed may be sent there—that is if he comes out single, so that we may not be separated so much another year. That was the original intention anyhow, when we first asked for Busteed, that he should be for Pyong Yang. We expect him now June 1st and from that time till after Annual Meeting, I hope he can get a good start at the language, and Doctor can go up with him and establish him early next fall. Of course it will be best for him not to remain much more than two months at a time perhaps or three.

This knocks a number of my calculations in the head. I had expected to take Esther with me there, and now I don't know just what is best to do with her. We think we have found her the right husband in the person of the Doctor's boy who he has had since last September and tested in the country and always found honest and reliable even in places where he could easily have been otherwise. He is 24 years old, tall, and good-looking, very gentle and modest in manners, blushes easily. He reads well in Korean and some in Chinese. We are going to send him to school two hours day, to study Chinese one hour and English the other. He is delighted with the idea of going to school, also with going to get such a good wife. We told him something about it yesterday, as Mrs. Scranton is in a hurry for Esther to marry. She is such a great big girl, and is seventeen now. The boy's name is 박유션이 [Yousan Pak]. He has given his name in on probation to Dr. Hall, and is really trying to be a faithful Christian. Esther, course, at present is far his superior, but she will no doubt help a great deal to make something of him, and he has it in him. Then he has a gentle loving heart and I am sure he will love her and she him when they come to know each other. He will probably send his "Sa Chu" or engagement paper May 1st and they'll likely be married within that month. May 1st is Esther's 17th birthday.

It seems strange to have my dear Esther marry. I had hoped for someone grander and greater, and had set up several idols for her, but one by one they fell—they were either lazy or dishonest. I have been praying now for more than a year that the Lord might send just the right man; and I believe he has. Esther, herself, can and will do much to make him a useful Christian man; and I am sure together they will do a great work for this people. God bless them.

> "Being perplexed, I say,
> Lord, make it right!
> Night is as day to Thee,
> Darkness as light.
> I am afraid to touch
> Things that involve so much.
> My trembling hand may shake,
> My skilless hand may break."[88]

---

[88] From "My Prayer" by an anonymous author.

Diary of Dr. Rosetta Hall 1892-1894

Monday, May 8, 1893

Who can find a virtuous woman? For her price is far above rubies. The heart of her husband doth safely trust in her, so that he hath no need of spoil. She will do him good and not evil all the days of her life. Prov. 31:10,11,12

> Heredity may count for much, but environment is next of kin to destiny.
> —Frances Willard's mother

I have had such a nice letter from Esther about the proposed marriage. It shows the consecration of the girl. It seems her mother was not pleased with the match when she heard that formally 유션이 [Yousanie] had been a 마부 [*mapoo*] or hostler, but after learning his father was a teacher (he died 5 years ago and his mother 6 years ago) that his two sisters had married farmers and were living in the country, that his youngest brother lived with one sister, and that 유션이 [Yousanie] being the eldest was compelled to go to work after the death of his father, though before that he had always gone to school and had mastered two books in Chinese, and knowing that now is the Doctors trusted boy, she has become reconciled. But Esther wrote me the following before the most of these things were known. No one could have blamed the girl if she too had felt badly about marrying a man from the lower class, as nearly everyone of the school girls have married into the higher class, and as I wrote last week, even I myself, was a bit disappointed; but this is the way this dear girl looks at it.

Diary of Dr. Rosetta Hall 1892-1894

"My very precious sister,

How are you today and is Dr. Hall quite well? I am well and happy. I was much pleased with your letter yesterday. You wrote to me very long and also say many strange words. Now I will tell you some strange words which I never tell. Do you know how my heart feel? Three nights I could not go to sleep and feel troubled, because I never like man, and also I do not know how to sew well; but Korean custom all girls have to marry, have to be wife and husband. I cannot help that, even I do not like man. If our dear Heavenly Father send Mr. Pak here and He make me for his wife I will be his wife. If God send me anywhere I will go. If God send him to be my husband then I shall be his wife though my mother do not like him, but my mother do not know him well. I tell my mother what use to find he is low or high. I tell many things to her. I tell her people who have no father and mother can do 마부 [mapoo or hostler] work if it is need. I do not care rich or poor or high or low. You know I will not get married to one who do not like Jesus word. I think it will be very very queer if I get married. My heart will get very much different. I say these funny words only to you. Please do not tell anybody. Please burn this up.

From your sister,

Esther Kim"

Dear Esther, what lessons of consecration she teaches me from day to day. I do love her.

Diary of Dr. Rosetta Hall 1892-1894

I trust now that Mr. Pak's environment is changing for the better that he will grow like Esther, and I believe he will. He has not had a chance heretofore, no more than she would have had if her father had not put her into Mrs. Scranton's school before he died. I believe in what Mrs. Willard says in the quotation for today; and now we will see if with a Christian wife and surrounded by Christian influences 박유션이 [Yousan Pak] will not make his mark in the world yet.

Tuesday, June 17, 1893

Surely goodness and mercy shall follow me all the days of my life. Psa. 23:6

> The child opens his eyes upon the wonder of the world, and comes to a knowledge of his powers little by little. In myself, I was never more a child, never more on the threshold of all possible good, than I am today. ++ The Power to comprehend only reveals more and more to comprehend. The power to enjoy but reveals more and more to enjoy. ++ If this may continue; if the way may still conduct me into higher sensations, into greater knowledge, into more divine love; if the future shall open and open; ++ if I may draw closer to better hearts, and draw out more of the fathomlessness of my being; if this may be, just step by step, little by little, —I shall not ask, for I cannot conceive, a more glorious destiny.
> —Herman Bisbee

Thank, there need to be no "if" about it, for He has promised "the Lord will give grace and glory. No good thing will He withhold from them that walk uprightly," (Ps.

Diary of Dr. Rosetta Hall 1892-1894

84:11) and "They that wait upon the Lord, shall renew their strength; they shall mount up with wings as eagles, they shall run and not be weary; and they shall walk, and not faint." (Isa. 40:31) Then there is that verse that dear Doctor so often quotes, "The path of the just is as the shining light that shineth more and more unto the perfect day." (Prov. 4:18)

This is the first anniversary of our wedding day. It seems so strange to each of us that we have been married a whole year—the time has flown so swiftly it is difficult to realize it. To each, it has been the happiest year by far of our lives. Doctor never tires of telling me how I have completed his happiness. He is so perfectly satisfied, and is ever expressing his great love both in the words and in "actions that speak louder than words"[89] and yet he wishes he could tell me more. If a year ago it was impossible for me to put into words my love for my Doctor, it is still more so today, but I can put it into actions better than then. Dear Doctor understands me, and I him, and we are so happy. The future looks so bright before us, though we little know even where our work shall lie another year, but that is in His Hands, as are we, and we feel sure wherever he leads is best. At present we are very comfortably situated in the house formerly occupied by Dr. McGill. We have our rooms upon one side and the Nobles upon the other, with hall, dining room, storeroom, and kitchen in common. We keep house together, just as before, Mrs. Noble house-keeper one month, and I the next. Dr. Busteed has been sent out upon Dr. Hall's and Mr. Noble's offer to pay his passage and

---

[89] Mark Twain, in *The Adventures of Huckleberry Finn*.

Diary of Dr. Rosetta Hall 1892-1894

support him the first year[90], so we are boarding him. We have been busy the last few days fixing up his rooms in the hospital building—they look quite cozy. We all like Dr. Busteed very much, and he is already quite one of the family. Mrs. Noble is housekeeper this month, and this evening she had a cake for supper beautifully frosted with the dates "1892, 1893" upon it, for us, and I had quite a large piece of the "Bride's Cake" of my wedding that I gave to each. I have yet more to keep—think I can keep some for the 5th or 10th anniversary, perhaps the 50th.

We continue to have good news from home—all well. In Mother's last letter she said, "When I wrote to Mr. Appenzeller about taking the package out to you, in his reply he said that 'Dr. Hall and his wife are good workers, and I feel it an honor to labor with such workers'" and mother adds, "Such as this is what makes us proud of our children." How glad we are that God helps us to please our dear parents in this way. Frank wrote me a nice letter not long ago. He spoke of seeing Father at Thanksgiving time, and that he seemed quite as well as ever then. Oh, I do trust we shall find them all there when we go home. I had

---

[90] William James Hall wrote in his 1892 annual mission report that if the Board would send a medical doctor to Pyong Yang, he would be responsible for the half of the salary for two years (see footnote 41). This proposal was accepted by the Board as written in the official letter dated February 23, 1893: "The proposition made by Dr. Hall and Brother Noble that if Dr. Busteed should be sent out, they would be responsible for his outgoing and for his support to the end of the year, 1893, was accepted and Dr. Busteed appointed as a medical missionary.(Letter from A. B. Leonadd to W. B. Scranton. Missionary Files: Methodist Episcopal Church; Board Correspondence, 1884-1915, Microfilm D3461, Reel 112, Letterbook 208).

Diary of Dr. Rosetta Hall 1892-1894

been speaking in my home letters that we might go to Pyong Yang to live this fall, and Mother wrote that now Dr. Cutler was here she thought I might come home even before my five years now that I was married, that I ought to come before settling down in the new place, and could just as well as not. Dear Mother, she doesn't think about how hard it would be for my dear husband. I have suggested something of the kind to him before now, and it just almost breaks his heart to think I might do it. He says I went away and left him once, and though he did bear it then, he feels he could not now.

I have opened work for women at the South Gate Dispensary[91] (where Dr. McGill was). Esther helps me. We only go two days a week, and then have service Sunday afternoon there. I continue the East Gate work, and am three days a week at the hospital. Dr. Cutler is there at the other three days. We are not having very much work anywhere as it rains nearly every day; the rainy season seems to have already begun. Dr. Hall was all ready to start for the country for another trip before annual meeting, but the day he expected to start it rained, and continued to for a week, and he is caught here in the rainy season instead of at

---

[91] South Gate Dispensary and Hospital was started by Dr. McGill in the fall of 1890. Rosetta opened the new woman's medical work at South Gate Dispensary in June 1893. In *1891 Annual Report of the Methodist Episcopal Church Foreign Missions*, 300 patients were seen at the South Gate Street Hospital in 1890, while the East Gate ("Aogi") Dispensary opened in 1889 "has been closed to medical work because of insufficient attendance to warrant the expenditure of time needed to go and come." For reference, the Woman's Hospital in Seoul (Po Ku Nyo Kwan) had seen 1,576 patients in 9 months, Chong Dong (the original and main place of work) Hospital 5,360 in 1890.

Diary of Dr. Rosetta Hall 1892-1894

Pyong Yang. I am so glad now seeing it has come so early that he did not get off when he expected. He has been working very hard, first attending to the repairs of this house, then of the College building which was in a very bad condition, of the McGill hospital, and Appenzeller house, the fences of the Mission in general, and also has done the medical work for Dr. Scranton most of the time; so it has not been until within the last a few days he could open a Korean book for study. That makes four months that he has not been able to do any studying since January; but I think from now on during the rainy season, we can both get more time. It is not a very good time to study however, as it is about all one wants to do to drag through with every day duties and exist. I have not begun to feel it very much though yet, as it has been quite cool; but today it has been so warm and moist, my whole body has been wet with perspiration all day. It seems strange that the rainy season should begin so early, but most people begin to think this is really it.

So ends our first year of married life. Both have surpassed in happiness, our highest dreams.

> "All dreams are not false; some dreams are truer than the plainest facts. ++ Let the dreamer only do the truth of his dream, and one day he will realize all that was worth realizing in it—and a great deal more and better. –George MacDonald
>
> "Keep true to the dreams of thy youth." [92]

---

[92] Friedrich Schiller.

Diary of Dr. Rosetta Hall 1892-1894

Wednesday, July 26, 1893 At 북한 (Pukhan)[93]

Above all things have fervent love among yourselves. I Peter iv. 8

> "The supreme happiness of life is the conviction that we are loved; loved for ourselves—say rather, loved in spite of ourselves."—Victor Hugo

Here we are living out of doors day and night upon top of Pukhan, the highest mountain near Söul. Doctor put up his Canadian tent upon a bold promontory overlooking a beautiful valley, and here we sleep at night, but through the day it is too warm here, and we spend most of the time in our hammocks under some beautiful shade trees near. We have most of our meals served out here, but occasionally take our breakfast in the tent. We brought our cook with us, and Doctor installed himself housekeeper, so I am relieved of all responsibility, and it is so nice. We are reading *Peep of Day*[94] in Korean together through the day—one of the books in our course. Doctor generally studies it aloud while I sew. Every evening we take a mountain climb together. Often Doctor stops me saying, "Give me a kiss my precious darling." Indeed, this seems like another honeymoon evermore sweet than the first—in short, our whole wedded life has been but one continues honeymoon, growing sweeter with each day. Doctor was telling me last evening that he used to, often in his bachelor days, feel so lonely and have an intense longing for someone or something he

---

[93] Bukhansan, or Bukhan Mountain, is a mountain on the northern peripheries of Seoul, South Korea.
[94] *The Peep of Day* by Favell Lee Mortimer.

scarcely understood what; he would think if he could but see his dear friend Omar Kilborn[95] it would be all right; but sometimes when with him he would have similar feelings, but now he says he is perfectly satisfied—he has not a longing but that is more than realized.

Our daily routine here is generally about like this. We arise at 6 a.m., take our baths, dress, and are ready for breakfast at 7 o'clock. We have a bowl of rice, eggs, bread and cocoa. Then we have our prayers, and later, Korean prayers with the cook and Doctor's teacher. We then read a little from Frances Havergal's[96] life if we have time before 9 a.m. when we begin studying Korean and continue this until 12 noon when we dine off of chicken, new potatoes, bread, and green corn, or cucumbers, sometimes desert of rice pudding, custard or tapioca pudding, but Doctor often forgets to order desert. We then read until 2 p.m. when we begin Korean again and study till 5 o'clock, then we meet with some other missionaries who are stopping in the Buddhist temple near us for the hot season, and we

---

[95] Omar Leslie Kilborn (1867-1920) was born in Frankville, Ontario near Kingston and was a childhood friend of William James Hall, who brought Omar into religion one evening at his home. Dr. Kilborn writes, "I was so fortunate as to have this man's influence thrown about me before he had been many months at school, and I shall praise God for it as long as I live." Dr. Kilborn graduated from the Medical College of Queen's University and sailed to China on October 4, 1891 to serve in Chengdu. He opened Western medical care to the region and founded the West China School of Medicine. While visiting his family in 1920, he died of pneumonia in Toronto.
(http://cschengdu.ca/?page_id=759)

[96] Frances Ridley Havergal (1836 –1879) was an English religious poet and hymn writer. *Take My Life and Let it Be* and *Thy Life for Me* (also known as *I Gave My Life for Thee*) are two of her best known hymns.

Diary of Dr. Rosetta Hall 1892-1894

have a Bible study together—we have taken up the subject of Christ's second coming. At 6 o'clock, we have supper, bean soup, potato soup, or chicken soup, bread, cake and canned fruit, after which Doctor makes the beds up for the night, and we take a walk, take our baths afterwards, and retire by 9 o'clock or before. So we are leading a very regular and orderly life if we do live out of doors all the time like gypsies and are becoming as brown as berries. We are just as happy as the days and nights are long. This morning after breakfast, Doctor said he had never felt so rested since he had been in Korea. I suppose we can have but one more week of this life, for then I must return to my work in Söul—am engaged to officiate at the birth of Mrs. Moore's child which is expected somewhere between the 1st of August and the 5th, and then Mrs. Swallen's about 10 days later, and perhaps of Mrs. Reynolds' another 10 or 15 days later, also perhaps Dr. Cutler who has been relieving me will need a little vacation, and as Annual Meeting begins about the 23rd it looks as if 2 weeks' vacation is all I shall be able to get this year. Well, I feel it will answer very well. I was feeling quite worn out the last week or two I was home; the nights were so hot I was unable to get much sleep; the work at the dispensaries was hardly as much as usual, but then it took about the same time, and I had more out-calls; and being engaged for these obstetric cases, we felt if I did not come now I could not at all, so we started right off. I had never tried tenting out before, but I like it very much and it seems to agree with me. I sleep very well, eat well, and already feel quite rested.

Diary of Dr. Rosetta Hall 1892-1894

One day Rev. Moore, Doctor, and I started out to climb to the top of "Sugar Loaf," a very high, smooth, bald mass of rocks facing us. It proved much farther away than we thought and we had of course to go around upon the other side in order to ascend it at all. We took no lunch with us and having eaten but a light breakfast we felt quite exhausted before we had reached the top. Mr. Moore started on for a still higher peak with some Koreas for pilots and he scaled its very apex. He has climbed a great deal among the Rockies, but says this was the most difficult fate he ever undertook. After resting a time, Doctor and I went on and accomplished what we had started out to do. We had a beautiful view of the Yellow Sea, the river, and all the surrounding country. We then descended, but oh, I got so tired before we reached our tent. It was noon and very warm and I was quite exhausted. I think if we had but a lunch with us it would have been alright. However, after dinner I quite quickly recovered, and the next day did not even feel stiff as I usually do after such a mountain climb.

Since leaving home the Lord has mercifully preserved me from injury in two dangerous falls. I came up on horseback and we had hardly gotten out of Söul before the saddle turned with me and I was thrown to the ground. It was in a great bed of mud and save some pretty dirty clothes I was not hurt. The other day, I was in a hammock that was hung very tight and somehow I suddenly turned myself out of it, and fell striking my head on a large stone. I had a headache from it the rest of the afternoon, and there are some bruises upon my arm but that was all. Doctor was quite frightened at first, both times, especially as I am nearly six-months (lunar) pregnant and it therefore seemed more serious.

That is the first I have written that about myself, and I have not told anyone. I think as yet no one has suspected it, but the doctor and myself. For some time it seemed impossible to realize, and even now it hardly seems true that I am so soon to be a mother, but I have felt the dear little thing moving about within me for several weeks now, and that seems to bring it nearer. I have been real well, troubled scarcely at all with either nausea or indigestion, and I have been able to carry on my work just as before, in fact, have started both the East Gate and South Gate dispensaries since in addition to the main hospital and dispensary. I have attended all sorts of cases surgical and otherwise, indeed performed that operation for scirrhus, removing the breast and axillary glands. I think it will not hurt me. I am not at all nervous about such things.

We are so thankful to our dear Heavenly Father that He is thus blessing our union. Doctor is so very fond of children, and thought of late years I have lost much of the interest I had as a girl and a teacher in children, no doubt it will revive at the coming of this little stranger, and not only revive but grow beyond anything I ever knew. I do so want the Lord to teach me how to be just one of the very best of mothers. I know Dr. Hall will be just one of the best of fathers as he is of husbands. We have consecrated the dear little one, from the very first, to our Lord, and trust we will never have any cause to regret thus clothing our love with form and immortality. We perhaps cannot realize its seriousness altogether , and yet I am sure we do in a measure, but our trust is in Him who so clearly brought us together, and we feel assured that "He doeth all things well."[97] He promises "As thy days, so shall thy strength to be." (Deut. xxxii. 25) Ourselves and all we have are His, and surely all that He sends to us shall be for His glory. Since that blessed relation of bride and wife has come to me I understand much better than I could before those passages in His dear Word that claims the Church as His bride, that he desires us without "spot or wrinkle, or any such thing"[98] that "Christ is the head of the church"[99] as "the husband is head of the wife"[100] and as it is right, seemly, and even a privilege, for the loving wife to be subject to her own husband "in everything"[101] so it is our loving privilege to be subject to Christ. When I think how great is the Doctor's love for me, and then think how Christ loves us with a divine love that must surpass that of husband, is seems too wonderful to comprehend. And, now, I am soon to understand more fully those precious passages in the Bible about mother-love. So, "slowly, by toil and pain, there has come to me a more sacred friendship, a deeper worship, a vaster thought, a more abundant delight."[102]

> O, great heart of God! whose loving
>   Cannot hindered be nor crossed;
> Will not weary, will not even
>   In our death itself be lost —
> Love divine! of such great loving

---

[97] Mark 7:37.
[98] Ephesians 5:27.
[99] Colossians 1:18.
[100] Ephesians 5:23.
[101] Ephesians 5:24.
[102] Herman Bisbee. See July 25, 1892 diary.

Diary of Dr. Rosetta Hall 1892-1894

> Only mothers know the cost —
> Cost of love which, all love passing,
> Gave a Son to save the lost.
> —Saxe Holm[103]

Wednesday, August 2, 1893

Turn away mine eyes from beholding vanity; and quicken thou me in thy way. Psa. 119:37

> "All things of this life are vanity if they are in contrast to the things of eternal life; but if they correlate the latter then they are but foretaste of heaven here below."
> —Rev. S. H. Scott in a sermon at Liberty, N. Y., 7-27-'90.

I expect this is our last day at Pukhan for this year, as all too quickly the two weeks have flown by.

Doctor went down to Söul last evening to urge Mr. and Mrs. Noble to come up and take our place today as we go down. We have tried to persuade them by letter ever since we have been here to do this, but everything has been without avail so far. We felt sort of responsible for their health, and think they need this change. If Doctor can't prevail upon them to come, I think he will at least bring Dr. Busteed back with him. Dr. Busteed has not seemed very robust since his arrival. I suppose he was over-worked in New York just as Doctor was. Dr. Scranton is away with his

---

[103] A pseudonym of Helen Hunt Jackson. See June 29, 1892 diary.

family at Chemulpo, so Dr. Hall will have to attend to the hospital now, otherwise he would remain up here with Dr. Busteed, and let me go home.

We had no rain until Monday, at night it rained real hard, but it did not come through our tent. We were as comfortable and "snug as a bug in a rug." It cleared off nicely yesterday afternoon, but very early this morning it rained the quite hard again. Just now it seems to be again growing clear, and it is very warm. I fear unless Doctor got an early start, he will have a pretty hard time coming up today. I staid all alone in our tent last night and was not afraid. The ladies over to the buildings said they would not have done it for anything, they would have been afraid of tigers, wild-cats and robbers. I have an idea that the Doctor worried about me a little when night came, but he didn't need to.

Mrs. Greathouse came up Monday to join the Vinton party at the buildings, quite an undertaking for a lady 75 years old. She is real well now.

I have a gotten all my correspondents answered up since I have been here, have darned a lot of socks and stockings, knit Doctor a pair of suspenders, and have done quite a lot of fancy work beside. We did not quite finish the reading of *Peep of Day* in Korean, but would have I think if the Doctor had not gone away.

I have had one letter from Mother since we have been up here. Poor Father has been suffering with his second attack of gout—it lasted three weeks. I am so sorry that he

Diary of Dr. Rosetta Hall 1892-1894

should have this trouble. He has always been so well and free from pain, it must be hard to bear, and then too at the same time his eyes were so affected that he could not read for his usual pastime. He was well again, before Mother closed her letter. Dear Mother, too, had had the most severe attack of heart-trouble she ever had, but recovered from it all right, thank God.

I am beginning to feel pretty uncomfortable at times from my size—feel the worst this morning I have at any time yet. Think I can't keep my secret from people's eyes much longer; believe the first chance I have upon my return to Söul I shall engage my doctor and nurse, Dr. Cutler and Miss Lewis. Doctor Hall thinks he will not be worth anything when his darling is sick and in pain, and we both like Dr. Cutler very much, and I prefer a woman doctor; we have agreed to put the whole case in her hands.

I wish Dr. Hall would hurry up and come back. I am getting lonesome without him, think I will write a little more to Mother to pass away the time.

Tuesday, September 19, 1893
Tuesday, September 19, 1865.

The anniversary of my birthday. In my Bible reading this morning the "text for the day" was a precious promise.

> "God shall be with you, and bring you again unto the land of your fathers." Gen. 48:21

Diary of Dr. Rosetta Hall 1892-1894

I see not a step before me,
    As I tread on another year;
But I've left the past in God's keeping, —
    The future His Mercy shall clear,
And what looks dark in the distance,
    May brighten as I draw near.

I know not what awaits me,
    God kindly veils mine eyes;
And o'ver each step of my onward way,
    He makes new scenes to rise;
And every joy He sends me, comes
    As a sweet and glad surprise.[104]

The day has been a quiet one, have helped Doctor in making his preparations for the country, as this is his last day with me for a time. He starts for Pyong Yang again tomorrow. Doctor put up our open grate stove for me today in the sitting room. We have not used it yet, but I think I shall like it very much. He has always been doing other little odd chores for my comfort during his absence. He says, "My darling wife, it is a great trial to leave you this time, but I commit you to God, and I know He will keep that which I have committed unto Him. As I have you from Him I believe He will have a special care over you." Dear Doctor, I am sure he is just one of the most loving husbands there ever was. I never expected to be blessed with such an amount of love. My own heart expands and responds to it, and we are so happy together.

---

[104] By Mary Gardiner Brainard.

Diary of Dr. Rosetta Hall 1892-1894

Mother's last letter said that they were all well at home. She began with,

> "Dear Children,
> The time has come around again for me to begin this chat with you. What a privilege it is to us all that we can converse in this way. Should we ever be deprived of it how unhappy we would be. It is so nice to hear from you so often, as Pa says we hear from you oftener than we do from Charles and Frank. I have gotten so I can almost tell when we will get your next. I don't think I ever miss a day but that I pray for all of you in the good work there in Korea. I hope a good Master will keep us all safe and well that we may meet again. Will it not be nice after being separated so long to again arrive at the old Home and see us all—only so much older?"

Dear mother, I wonder what she will say when she hears of the dear little coming one—she knows nothing about it yet. But I have written in my last letter, so she will know in about five weeks now. I told her I expected it about the time of Father's birthday, November 10. How nice it would be if it might come that very day.

Since I last wrote, the Annual Meeting has been held. Bishop Foster[105] presiding. Dr. Leonard[106], Conference Secretary, and Mrs. Keen[107], Branch Secretary of the W. F. M. S., were with us. I was able to report that during the

---

[105] Bishop R. S. Foster, D.D.
[106] Adna Bradway Leonard, D.D., LL.D. was Corresponding Secretary of the Board of Foreign Missions of the Methodist Episcopal Church from 1888 to 1912, died in 1916. *The Christian Advocate*, April 27, 1916.
[107] Mrs. J. F. Keen.

Diary of Dr. Rosetta Hall 1892-1894

past year I had treated 6260 cases, 2125 were dispensary patients first visits, 3495 were their return visits, 531 were calls to patients in their homes, and 119 were cared for in the hospital wards. The aggregate number of cases treated during my 3 years here is over 14,000. Though the real spiritual fruit of this work has as yet appeared small, yet we praise God for the small beginnings He permits us to see, trusting they are but the promises of a richer harvest by and by. Each of the five promising converts spoken of in last year's report have been received into the church this year, and art active in trying to bring others to Christ; and among the baptized probationers this year, there are at least four who first became interested through what they heard at the hospital. I would like to quote more from my report[108], but will not take the time.

Dr. Hall and I are both appointed to Pyong Yang this year, and for that we are very thankful, though I suppose I shall not be able to go there before next spring. How nice it will be when the way so opens there that we can make it our home.

Dr. Scranton is continued in the office of Superintendant. Rev. Appenzeller is Treasurer and in the Boy's Col-

---

[108] See Rosetta's article on the Chinese Recorder, April 1894 (Appendix 6).
Twenty-fourth Annual Report of the Woman's Foreign Missionary Society for the Year 1892-1893 only recorded Dr. Mary Cutler's report briefly, but did not include Rosetta's report. Seventy-fifth Annual Report of the Missionary Society of Methodist Episcopal Church for the Year 1893 only reported men's medical work: "total number of patients at dispensary, 5,087; total number of new patients at dispensary 2,692."(p 254)

Diary of Dr. Rosetta Hall 1892-1894

lege[109], Rev. Ohlinger is home on leave, as is also Miss Rothweiler. Rev. and Mrs. Jones go to Chemulpo, Dr. McGill continues his work at Won San, and Rev. Noble in the Boy's College, also pastor at Ioge[110]. Rev. Hulbert appointed to Press work. Dr. Busteed to hospital work here in Dr. Scranton's hospital, Dr. Cutler and Miss Lewis in my hospital. Miss Paine in the two new ladies, Misses Harris[111] and Frey[112] to school work, Mrs. M. F. Scranton in charge of Woman's Work and the Home. I think everyone is pleased with the appointments. We had a very delightful session, altogether.

I continued the work in the hospital till about September 10th to give Dr. Cutler a little rest, as she got a little fogged out during my 2-week vacation at Pukhan, and soon after the two obstetric cases Mrs. Moore and Mrs. Swallen took a great deal of my time so that Dr. Cutler helped me

---

[109] Pai Chai College

[110] Aogi Church, modern day Ahyun Methodist Church in Seoul, was established by Dr. William B. Scranton on December 12, 1887, pastored by Rev. Ohlinger until Rev. Noble took over in 1893. http://ahyun.net.

[111] Miss Mary W. Harris came to Korea in 1893 for educational work, married Rev. E. Douglas Follwell, M.D. in 1897, and served in Pyong Yang until 1920. Her sister, Dr. Lillian N. Harris (1863 – 1902), later came to Korea as a medical missionary in 1897 and served with Rosetta at the East Gate Hospital and Pyong Yang Extended Grace Hospital; she died of typhus fever during her service in Pyong Yang in 1902 and was buried at the bank of Dae-Dong River. The East Gate Hospital was later named the Lillian Harris Memorial Hospital.

[112] Miss Lulu E. Frey (1968–1921) came to Korea in 1893 for educational work and served as the fourth principal of Ewha Girls' School from 1907 to 1920. She went home on furlough in 1920, but died of cancer in America the next year.

Diary of Dr. Rosetta Hall 1892-1894

out at the hospital. However, I have stopped most of my work now, except a few out-calls now and then or to help Dr. Cutler in on operation. I am in hopes of making good use of the [postpartum] time I can get this coming winter in the study of the language, as the best preparation I can make for Pyong Yang work.

Just now I am beginning to get into that perfectly new work for me—making "baby's clothes." It doesn't seem so strange after all as I thought it would—it just sort of seems as if I were set back 20 years, and was again making my doll's clothes, of which I used to be very fond, and now I find I enjoy this work also. My Korean woman who does our room work and darning and mending, etc. comes in very good now to do the hand-sewing. I sew up all the seams upon the machine, but I have taught her to make button-holes, and a fancy stitch, and she hems very neatly anyhow, so she does all of the finishing up which takes the longest time anyhow. I like this woman, "Chemo[113]" I call her, very much; she is a splendid little worker. I have never had my work done so well since I've been in Korea, as by her. She is so pleased to know that I am expecting a little baby, and takes fully as much pride as I do in making the little clothes. I think she will make a lovely nurse for the baby. I'd like to write more of what I am making, but must not take the time. I am only making what I think will really be necessary, and am putting no more work upon them than to make them neat, though most of them do look pretty also.

---

[113] Seamstress.

Diary of Dr. Rosetta Hall 1892-1894

"Oh, the sweetest work a mother knows
Is making the baby's dainty clothes."

Friday, November 10 1893

Now let thy words come to pass. How shall we order the child, and how shall we do unto him? Judg. 13:12

"New-born baby, soft and pink
Of the two worlds on the brink."

It is all over with, and my baby is here. Just to think he came on the very day I had wished for him, his grandfather Sherwood's birthday. He is a great big boy of nine pounds, born at 10 a.m. of the 10th day of the 10th moon, and his name is <u>Sherwood Hall</u>.

I have been so well all the time. Only yesterday I made five out-calls on Korean patients, one away over near Mrs. Greathouse's on the wife of her house-boy "Sue." They were married just a little after we were, and about ten days ago a little baby came to them. As Mrs. Sue is only a girl of sixteen or seventeen, and she had no medical assistance, she was quite badly torn; and they sent for me yesterday to see if I could help her, which I think I can do. I cleaned the wounds and made the necessary applications and taught her mother-in-law how to continue the treatment, and said I'd see her again Monday, but suppose I will not now.

Doctor went with me, and as we didn't start until after we got through studying at 4 o'clock, it got dark before I

Diary of Dr. Rosetta Hall 1892-1894

was through, and as it threatened rain also, we hurried home and got there just in time for supper. As it was prayer meeting night, and I had another patient to give a douche to yet, I didn't stay to prayers. I got through my work just 7:30 p.m., in time for the meeting, which later resolved itself into the regular semiannual meeting of the Union Church, for which I as Secretary and Treasurer had to read two reports. Got home and to bed about 10 o'clock. Of course I felt a little tired, and my back ached, but that was nothing new. However, as the next day was to be father's birthday, I spoke of it to Doctor, and how that was the day I had hoped our baby would come, but now that the time was so near I dreaded it more and more, and somehow I felt a little nervous and anxious. Doctor tried to comfort me, be reminding me how bravely I had stood operations on my neck without ether and all, but I told him I was not so brave as I used to be I was sure, and then we went to sleep. About 3 a.m., I awoke as I often did in the night, and I spoke of feeling a little pain to the Doctor, then I got almost asleep again, when the pain returned. It was not much but just enough, and often enough to prevent me from getting to sleep. After a little I said to Doctor, "Why, I believe I am really in labor. You better get up and light the light." He did so, and I tried to get up too, and get a few things in place, but labor came on so fast I had to get back in bed pretty soon. And Doctor scarcely had time to get the little iron bed, which I wanted to be sick on, brought in and ready. He had to ask Mr. Noble to send for Dr. Cutler and Miss Lewis. Dr. Cutler came at 8 o'clock, and Miss Lewis just after the baby came. Of course they both supposed as I had, that being 28 years old and my first baby, I would not be in a hurry about it. However it was all over in six hours. I had a great deal of pain in my back, but otherwise I did not suffer very much. Poor Doctor, he was so anxious for me, and when my temperature went up to 102° at night and pulse 130, he feared a hemorrhage so that he couldn't go to sleep though Miss Lewis stayed with me and the baby. Miss Lewis laughed at the Doctor, she had heard him return thanks with me to our Father for answering our early morning prayer to give me a safe and a speedy delivery and then he had prayed that I might soon be restored to my wanted health and strength, so Miss Lewis says, "What's the matter, Doctor, can't you trust the Lord? Where is your faith?" Poor dear precious husband, he was so tired and distracted, I fear he had not thought whether he had faith or not. However, I got through the night all right—the high temperature and pulse seemed to be due to "surgical shock" as you might say only.

How wonderfully the Lord has fulfilled the precious promise He gave me on my wedding day.

> "I will bring the blind by a way that they knew not; I will lead them in paths that they have not known: I will make darkness light before them, and crooked things straight. These things will I do unto them, and not forsake them. Isa. xlii. 16

And the dear little boy baby, "Our Baby," was its mother's first greeting to it when she asked to see him before ever he had been washed. He seemed like a patient little fellow even if he did seem to be in a hurry to try his new life in this cold world, for he only cried once just enough to

Diary of Dr. Rosetta Hall 1892-1894

let us know he was living and had a good pair of lungs, and then he was very quiet the rest of the day. He is not pretty, his nose is large for a baby and his features are "all boy." I used to think all of babies looked alike, but no one would mistake him for a girl baby at least. No doubt he will grow better looking as he grows older as John Ely Moore has done, he was a homely baby too when born, looked very much like my baby, but now at 3 months he is as beautiful a baby as one would wish to see.

Sherwood has true blue eyes that look very beautiful to me even if they have something of the oriental slant of many of the Korean eyes. He has a good mouth, and good-looking ears; his forehead is a bit low now, but he has a large well shaped head. He has the prettiest finger nails that I ever noticed, but I suppose that is because I never noticed baby-nails much. His fingers are surely like his father's, though his hand looks more like mine. He has a long well shaped body, but is not fat. Of course like all fond mothers as he is a boy I'd like him to look like his father, and I believe he will, in time, though at present he surely resembles no one but his own little self. Dear little Sherwood, how my heart goes out in love to him, how strangely sweet it seems when he nurses me. Miss Lewis thinks his Papa doesn't take enough notice of him, but he will after a little when he gets over being so anxious about me.

A mother's love begins to grow long before she sees her child. When she feels the new little life moving within her, next to her own heart, and when she is busy making the "baby's clothes," the mother-love cannot help but to grow, and thus she gets the start of the father; but for the first week or two after birth he has a rather more of the care and responsibility of the little life than the mother, and it is then that his love begins to take root, and like the mother's to grow and to live forever. I am so glad that Love is eternal. God in His Word saith, "Love never faileth."[114]

How thankful we are for this little "incarnation of the smile of God" upon our love. How we desire that He who has entrusted him to our care shall give us wisdom to train him for Him.

> "For this child I prayed; and the LORD hath given me my petition which I asked Him: Therefore I also have granted him to the LORD; as long as he liveth he is granted to the LORD. And he worshipped the LORD there. I Sam. i. 27, 28

Tuesday, February 6, 1894, Korean New Year's Day

And we know that all things work together for good to them that love God, to them who are called according to his purpose. Rom. viii. 28

> "Through long days that anguish,
>   And sad nights, did Pain
> Forge my shield, Endurance,
>   Bright and free from stain.
> Doubt, in misty caverns,
>   'Mid dark horrors sought,
> Till my peerless jewel,

---

[114] 1 Corinthians 13:8.

Diary of Dr. Rosetta Hall 1892-1894

<u>Faith</u>, to me she brought.
<u>Strife</u> that racked my spirit
  Without hope or rest,
Left the blooming flower,
  <u>Patience</u>, on my breast.
<u>Suffering</u> that I dreaded,
  Ignorant of her charms,
Laid the fair child, <u>Pity</u>,
  Smiling in my arms."
  — Adelaide Anne Procter

It has been so long since I have taken time to write in my journal that I am afraid there is too much to write for one day, but I will try and do the best I can at it.

My Korean teacher does not come today, of course. No Korean thinks he can do any work on New Year's Day, and most of them think the same for the following two weeks.

We continue to have good news from home, both from my home and from Doctor's home. All keep well and happy. We have had no letters as yet in the reply to ours telling of the baby, but I think next mail will bring them. I have had several letters from Mother since she knew about the expected baby. She learned it a little over a month beforehand, and from that time until she could get Doctor's letter sent, the first mail after baby's coming, would be about three months. I disliked keeping Mother thinking about it so long before she could hear the result, but was afraid she might not like it if I didn't tell her at all beforehand. However, she writes October 5th,

Diary of Dr. Rosetta Hall 1892-1894

> "Your last letter told us of the coming little new commoner. For my part, I would rather not have heard of it till after it was born; but as your sister says, you were so proud of it you couldn't help to tell us."

Now I deny the truth of sister's assertion. Not that I was not proud of it, but that was not the reason I told them. But because I thought they'd feel a little hurt if I didn't, and I believe they would have, and that after all they are glad they didn't have to wait till baby was 6 weeks old before hearing anything about him. In Mother's November letter, writing upon the very day baby came, she says,

> "Just told your Pa, this was his birthday. He says 'I don't see any presents.' I told him, 'Probably, they were on the road.'"

They little thought that meant a brand-new grandson born in distant Korea. It will be pleasant news I think when they learn it. Mother also says,

> "I suppose by the time you get this, you will have that child named or did you do that before it was born? You may kiss it once a day for me right through all you come home with it, then, I will do it myself."

In her last letter, December 11th, she says,

> "I hope the little one is well, and is a comfort to you both. Suppose it will not be long now before we will get the news about the dear child. We want all the particular, how much it weighs and circumference and so on."

Diary of Dr. Rosetta Hall 1892-1894

In one of Mother's recent letters, she wrote something that helps to set Doctor's heart at rest, and rather surprised me. It was this.

> "You spoke in one of your letters that you might possibly come Home alone without your husband. Of course we would be glad to see you, but we don't think it best for you to undertake such a thing without his help and company. We want the <u>whole</u> family when the time comes around so you can both leave."

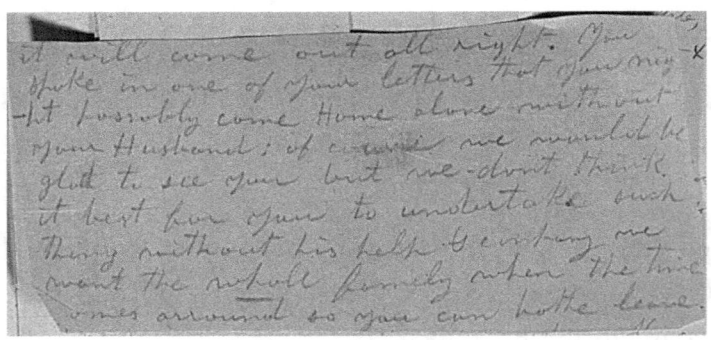

A clip from Mother's Letter

Well, this is a relief to me also. When I left home, as they only expected me to be gone five years, and Mother at least didn't want me to marry, I had thought that they would feel pretty bad to think that my marriage prevented me coming for a much longer time than that, and besides Mother wrote once she thought I ought to come home before settling in Pyong Yang. Well, well, how we all do change. Before I came to Korea, Mother thought I was quite capable of taking the long strange journey alone, that there was no need for a husband to care for me; but already you

Diary of Dr. Rosetta Hall 1892-1894

see, she thinks I can't even come home alone. Well, I feel much the same myself, and as I said before, it is a relief to me and a satisfaction to Doctor to learn that the dear home-folks look at it in this light.

All of these are pleasant things, but there have been also some hard things during the past 3 months.

When baby was three weeks old, Doctor started again for Pyong Yang. I had made a good recovery apparently, and baby seemed all right, except that he was unable to have his bowels moved without an enema each time. He had gained one pound, so we felt although it was hard that it was all right for Doctor to go. However, that night before, baby didn't seem at all well—wanted to nurse all the time, when as before he never nursed more than once and sometimes not at all during tonight. In the morning, he vomited some for the first; but though it helped to make my heart more than usually sad at the Doctor's going, yet neither one of us thought of it being more than a passing trouble. However, he kept growing worse all day, began to have loose tools also, and seemed to suffer so much pain. For quite two weeks, he was unable to retain more than two or three nursings upon the average for 24 hours, and sometimes along at first he had as many as 12 stools during that time, later he became constipated again, and could only have his stools after an enema, crying for hours sometimes in pain for want of one, and I'd not be sure whether it was that or what was the matter. Almost every night he had to go to sleep upon nothing but hot water, after his stomach had had a rest of six hours or so from food he would often keep down a nursing all right, or soon after a stool, but

Diary of Dr. Rosetta Hall 1892-1894

time and time again, he would throw up the whole nursing, crying in great pain until he got it all up. I tried everything I could think of, being very careful in my diet, even going without fresh fruit or fruit of any kind, which I don't believe in, but I felt quite like doing anything. I gave him lime water, bismuth and pepsin, barley water, etc., of course not all at the same time, but gave each a trial. He would retain them as he did my milk at times, but at other times would throw them up also as fast as I could keep them. He looked so pitiful, so tired and weary, and I would just feel as if he couldn't stand it, and oh, such a terrible three weeks I never want to put in again. At the end of that time, he weighed less than 9 pounds, had lost the pound he gained the first three weeks and more; so I knew he was really seriously ill. Oh, how I longed for his father, someone to share the responsibility with me, someone to sympathize with me and comfort me.

I look back now upon those three weeks as a perfect agony by day and terror by night. I was so foolish to have no one to help me beside Amah[115] who had her hands quite full with attending to my room work, the stove, the baby's washing, and ironing. She was as faithful as she could be and rested me from the baby all she could, but she worked so hard in the day, of course I couldn't think of keeping her nights. What I ought to have done was to have gotten another Amah for nights and to help when Amah No. 1 was washing and ironing which took four days a week. I wouldn't have gotten so tired and worn out, and baby would have gotten well much quicker, I am convinced, for

---

[115] A housemaid or children's nurse or nanny.

of course when he was sick and restless, I would be not only deprived of rest, but very anxious and then after the next nursing he would likely be worse, then I'd feel worse, and then again it would react, and I don't know what would have become of us if Doctor had not come home then at the end of the three weeks. The baby began to get better at once—had only one bad night after his Papa's return and little by little got so he could retain nearly every nursing providing he had about a half ounce of water either before or after it. At the end of the next week, he weighed no more, but weighed no less. At the end of the following week, he had gained a half pound, and now seems to be upon the uphill track again, though I have to be very careful about his nursings. He still has acid stools, and cannot pass them without an enema. But when he feels well, he is very sunny-hearted, laughing and cooing at you, and will lie in his basket playing with his fingers, which he seems to admire almost as much as his mama does, or he will play with a bone ring tied with a blue ribbon to the side of the basket, knocking it with his hand to hear it rattle against the side of the basket.

Caring for Sherwood so much night and day those three weeks when I was not very strong, brought in my old back ache again. It aches just as it used to when I was from 12 to 14 years of age, and the curvature of the spine was taking place. It still continues, sometimes, it feels as if some of the bones must drop out they hurt so. Amah gives it a good rubbing night and morning, and it is growing better now. Well, I am sure I can sympathize with mothers with sick babies as I never knew how to before. How many there are

Diary of Dr. Rosetta Hall 1892-1894

who have things much harder than I, and know much less what to do for the poor little suffering baby, I am sure doctor and all as I am, I felt helpless enough often times. How I pity those who are yet more helpless.

Doctor had scarcely been home a week, had just got into regular work on the language again, and expecting to continue it through the coldest winter months, as I think during the past year the most real studying he has been able to do was the two weeks we were at Pukhan, and the few weeks after his return in the Fall from Pyong Yang until baby came, the rest of the time has been taken up with his country trips, and attending to repairs on the school building, hospital, fences, etc. Well, as I say, he had no more than got a chance to begin study again, when he went to see Dr. Scranton one day, and was speaking about getting Kim Chang Sikey[116] and family moved up to Pyong Yang sometime in March, when Dr. Scranton exclaimed, "Don't you intend to make another trip before that time?" Doctor replied, "Why you don't expect me to travel this time of the year, do you doctor?" (We had been having very cold weather for a week or two with the promise of more.) Dr. Scranton said, "Yes, why not? That is your appointment. There is where your work is. You are getting your pay for that, and here you are here." Doctor said he

---

[116]Rev. Chang-Sik Kim (1857-1929) was born in Su-An, Hwanghae Province. While wandering around the country, he heard the Gospel through Mr. Ohlinger and became a Christian at age 30. After Ohlinger returned to China, he became William Hall's Helper and assisted the pioneer mission work in Pyong Yang. He was the first ordained Methodist minister in Korea and mainly served in the northern region. He suffered a stroke in 1922 and died in 1929. His extensive evangelistic work gained him a nickname "Korean Paul."

Diary of Dr. Rosetta Hall 1892-1894

felt he was doing as good work as he could in putting his time on the language. Dr. Scranton said, "Yes, your position in the Mission is a critical one, if you do not get this language soon you'll likely be sent where you don't need to use it." Poor Doctor, he was so hurt, surprised and grieved to be talked to in this way, he didn't know what to do or to say or what to understand by it. At any rate, he gathered this much that the Superintendant meant him to take another trip this winter, and he determined to do it. He came home to tell me all about it, but he felt so hurt at being treated in such a manner he couldn't trust himself to tell me, and went out again. In the evening, he told me. I could scarcely believe that Dr. Scranton had talked that way—could see no excuse for it. Poor Doctor, I never knew him to feel so badly over anything in his life, after working as hard and as faithful in opening up work in the interior as he had, then to be treated like a little boy in this manner. However, we knelt together and prayed over it, asking the Lord to make it a blessing, and not allow us to make it a curse to us, and after a while we felt better and set about making the preparations for a winter trip. However, we could see no excuse for exposing one's self in this weather and at the miserable inns where this time of year there is but one warm room, and coolies and *mapoo*s and everybody have to huddle together in the same room. When Doctor came down just before Christmas he had slept or tried to sleep with from 11 to 13 others in one small closed room. The work at Pyong Yang was not needing him, not nearly so much as he needs to study. On his last trip, he had found everything all right there, and could see no reason why we would not be able to go up together early in the spring and try living there. In the meantime, there seemed to be nothing in particular to be gained by another trip, and there was the two weeks' time at least to be lost from study upon the way there and back, besides of course he cannot study there as at home. There are so many sightseers to claim one's time. However as I say, he set about going as soon as possible—thought he could get off in another week anyhow.

In the meantime, Dr. Scranton called one day, and spent quite a little time talking about how much things should be "fixed up" at Pyong Yang before I went there to live, and that of course the Superintendant would expect a good room when he came to visit us, etc. Nothing important was said, Doctor answering yes to what he said, but of course supposing as he had opened the work, he would be allowed his own judgment in the matter as to how much "foreign fixing up" would be safe. However, the next Sunday, Dr. Scranton visited my Korean service for women at the South Gate, and walked home with me, and began asking me about what repairing and building and what furniture etc. Doctor was planning upon. I saw he meant to get out of me all he could, and also that if I didn't tell him something he would feel we were keeping back things he ought to know. So I told him the Doctor felt we should go very slow at first, and not alarm the people with building or with many foreign things, and make them think we had to really come for good, that it was less than a year ago they had put out the Presbyterian men from there, and it would be too bad to lose all the confidence Doctor had again been able to gain in the meantime, by being too rash,

Diary of Dr. Rosetta Hall 1892-1894

now. I said as we had planned it, at first, Doctor would go up with Chang Sikey's family in March, have new paper put on the rooms in the present house there, fresh matting, etc. and leave Chang Sikey in charge, and then we would go up taking a bed and a few chairs, but not much else, as there was a cook stove and some cooking utensils already there, and we thought for a month or two, we could get on very nicely, and then if all went well, we could plan our repairs together for doing in the fall, or even some perhaps in the spring if it seemed well so to do at the time. Well, Dr. Scranton thought this wouldn't do at all—that I never could live that way. I told him I lived two weeks on Pukhan last summer in a tent last summer in a tent without either chairs, table or a bed, and I enjoyed it very much; and if it were for the good of the work I could get along most anyhow for a time.

However, I saw he was not pleased, and his parting words to me were that "the Doctor must build, and that before summer, and if we couldn't live there someone else would." I wanted to say if Doctor and I, who are willing to put up with anything and everything, are not able to live there, I don't see who else could live there any better; however, I held my tongue. But when I told Doctor about it he feared I had talked altogether too much, but I assured him I said no more than I could help, and I didn't and I tried to put it all in the best way I could to please his majesty, the Superintendant. However, the next morning Dr. Scranton called a meeting of the building committee, and sent for Dr. Hall. Dr. Hall is on the committee but being only one of the three present thought it best not to disagree

Diary of Dr. Rosetta Hall 1892-1894

with them, it could do no good anyhow. So he was ordered to build a house 36 x 16 with eaves 2 feet and height from floor to rafters at eaves of 8 feet, stone foundation, etc., and to build a kitchen in addition if necessary to "take no account of any buildings on the place." Then they ordered him to get the following furniture in addition to what we have: "1 iron bed (full)—mattress, springs, and pillows $75, dressing bureau and wash stand $18, chairs $5, for bedroom; for dining-room, they ordered dining table $20, sideboard $15, stove $15; for sitting room and library, bookcase $14, table, chairs and c $52."; and with the orders to "furnish the three rooms at once." Well, we can't understand at all why the Superintendent should see fit to it act in this way, as though the Doctor's judgment was not to be taken at all about his own work, and about a work that Dr. Scranton has never even seen. It just looks as if he wanted to get the Doctor in trouble in some way if not in one way in another, as though he wanted him to disobey him. He said to the Doctor, "You can appeal to the Bishop if you like." I suppose he would, but it is practically of no use for the rule is "appeal to the Bishop but in the meantime, submit to the Superintendent." So as the Superintendent orders things to be done before there could be time to write and explain matters to America and receive reply that is of no use, and I suppose Dr. Scranton realized that.

There was one factor, however, that Dr. Scranton didn't take into account, that is, Dr. Hall is British Consul. Of course when Doctor goes into the Interior he has to obtain his passport of the British Consul, and he has always conferred more or less with him as to how far he could go in

Diary of Dr. Rosetta Hall 1892-1894

Pyong Yang, and be protected, and it was partly from his advice that we had concluded it best to go no faster than what I had told Mr. Scranton. Mr. Wilkinson the present Counsel is a very fine gentleman, has had much experience of the kind in China, and he is in hearty sympathy with Doctor opening up the work there. So Doctor went to him and asked his advice about his doing so and so. The Counsel would listen to nothing of the kind, said it would be most disastrous to the work, and that he could not support him nor protect him in anything of the kind as yet. He had no right to, but said we should go in there as though we were soon to leave, and in fact, we should leave soon the first few times, until we saw that the people wanted us, and as we were both doctors he thought this would soon be the case, and then he would feel like asking permission of the Government for us to reside there. But in the meantime, we should ever be ready to move out with a moment's warning, if only to go to another town for a short time and return. He said there could be no thought of building or taking in that amount of furniture, he felt sure the American Consul would feel the same about it. He would see and talk to him, and if necessary they would send for Dr. Scranton and inform him. I don't know whether they did or not, but probably it was unnecessary as he would at once see after Doctor told him (which he did do at once) that he could do nothing further at present. Of course he was very much put out, and told Doctor he "had no business to go to his Consul about it, and it was very difficult for him to do anything with both the Doctor and his Consul working against him." Why, bless his heart. Doctor never has thought of working against him, he only has the real advancement of the work at heart, and cannot bear to see all that he has with so much patience accomplished in over a year's work now, all brought to naught, and the work setback for no telling how long. Someone has suggested to Dr. Scranton it might be well for him to visit Pyong Yang himself this winter, and as during the conference year he has not only to visit Pyong Yang, but We Chu and Won San according to the Bishop's orders, and has made none of these visits yet, he will really have to be about it in order that it may all be accomplished before the rainy season. Someone said he was told to visit each place twice, but he can't do that now. It is already too late in the year.

Well, now to look back upon it and to write it coldly out, it doesn't seem so bad as at the time, but during those days Doctor and I felt so much troubled and puzzled to understand why we were treated thus. We see now a little better how it must have been next to impossible and indeed impossible for Dr. McGill and Mr. Olinger to get along with Dr. Scranton, for if anyone can get along with difficult people it is Dr. Hall. I never dreamed of his having trouble with anyone; and this is the first experience of the kind he ever had, and it is so hard upon him—why do you know he wants to leave the mission, he says, and it does look so, that for some reason Dr. Scranton has gotten prejudiced against him, and that he fears he will never let him alone until he gets him sent home like he has Mr. Ohlinger, and even if it should be short of that, he doesn't see how he can work to advantage always hampered and treated in this manner. He actually contemplates offering his services to the Pres-

Diary of Dr. Rosetta Hall 1892-1894

byterians, he says it don't matter about creed or doctrine, he is here to work for Jesus, and he must do it, if Dr. Scranton will not let him in this Mission, then he must get out; and I had all I could do to persuade him not to make propositions of that nature to Mr. Moffett at once upon his arrival in Pyong Yang. I know they would be only too glad to get Dr. Hall, and it would be a good lesson as to how some people in this Mission have been treated by the Superintendent. But I just think it would be awful, and it makes me feel so bad to think of it. And yet I don't want to see Doctor troubled as he has been of late.

Altogether these last three months have been difficult ones, and things have looked pretty dark, but I believe brighter days are coming. A week ago, Dr. Scranton did really start for Pyong Yang, and I think when he has actually traveled in the country more himself and has seen something of the work, he will be more reasonable.

I have been more fortunate than usual in hearing from Doctor often this time, for a while I had a letter every day, he would just happen to meet someone coming to Söul; and already I have received two letters from him since he reached Pyong Yang. Mr. McKenzie[117], a new missionary who just recently came from Nova Scotia went up with the Doctor, and he finds him a very congenial companion. I am so glad Doctor had company. He doesn't like solitude; it is much harder for him to bear than for me. Before I knew Doctor it was no punishment to me, but I rather think he

---

[117] Rev. William J. McKenzie, a Canadian missionary, arrived in Korean in 1893 and died on June 23, 1895.

Diary of Dr. Rosetta Hall 1892-1894

never enjoyed it. It is such a comfort to hear from often. I have also been able to send letters quite often. Here are some quotations from his letters.

> "Well, darling, I hope you have had a good night rest, and that you and Sherwood are feeling well this morning. I have left you both with God and I am sure He will take good care of you. Lean heavily upon Him my darling. It is such a comfort to get when we can trust Him for everything. He is teaching us some good lessons now. We will cheerfully and patiently learn them for I am sure good will come out of them for us. You are so precious to me darling, how dearly I love you. My love grows stronger for you every day, and for little Sherwood. When our home is so happy we must not let the little things of life disturb us. Don't worry about anything, but leave it all with Jesus. God has promised to keep them in perfect peace where mind is stayed on Him. I would like to bear the burdens for you, but our dearest friends come far short of being able to give us the needed comfort and help, but <u>Jesus</u> can, and praise the Lord, <u>He does</u>. I believe this trip will prove blessing to each of us, and let us cheerfully do hard things for Jesus. How my heart goes out in love to you. I am so thankful for such a precious wife to give my love to and to receive love from. And little Sherwood, dear little boy, he is getting very closely entwined around our hearts. I hope God may spare him to grow up to be a good man, a comfort and a joy to us, and a blessing to the world."

Diary of Dr. Rosetta Hall 1892-1894

March 10, 1894

Your heavenly Father knoweth what things ye have need of. Matt. vi. 8

> "Across the discord of our lives comes lowly
> One harmony our hears too seldom heed,
> The comfort given us by the Teacher holy:
> 'He knoweth ye have need.'"[118]

Sherwood is 4 months old today, and he weighs 12 pounds, is 24 inches long, circumference of cranium 15¾ inches. He is quite well now, though he doesn't get fat like Max Scranton who now weighs 18 pounds, yet he looks so much better than he did, I am sure his Papa can scarcely realize it is the same boy when he comes. He enjoys being talked and laughed to, and talks and laughs back at a great rate. He enjoys a big rag doll that is dressed in Korean boy's clothes. He will amuse himself with it while lying in his bed for a long time; also with shaking a Korean rattle that my teacher ought for him one day. If Amah pulls his bottle out of his mouth if he is hands are upon it he will put it back as fast as she can pull it out. He is just beginning to put out his hands to go to you if you ask for them. I think that is about all of the accomplishments he has, and I don't know how it compares much with other babies of that age, as I never before have had occasion to see much of babies. I should suppose however on account of his having been sick so long it is no more if as much as he ought to do. Taking into consideration that he has suffered to so much, I

---

[118] From "He Knoweth Ye Have Need" by Ellie A. Jewett.

think he is a pretty good boy because she has contracted as yet no bad habits, he does not cry to be carried, or to be rocked, in fact he is more sure to go to sleep if just laid down quietly in his bed at the proper time and fixing his milk so he can get it. He doesn't suck his thumb, or a "mother's comfort" or anything of that sort, he never soils his napkins, but has his stool each morning over a little Korean "*yokang*"[119] I bought for him. For the last week, for the first almost in his life, his stools are alkaline in reaction that makes me think that he is surely getting in a much more nearly normal condition. He still needs the enema however, but gets along with little or no pain, and does not have to strain and bear down so much as he used to. I still continue to nurse q.i.d.[120]—after breakfast, after Tiffin, after supper, and once in the night. He seldom wakes up more than once at night that will be as a rule somewhere between 12 and 2 o'clock, he then nurses from a half to one hour and goes to sleep again until 6 or 7 a.m. My milk keeps up about the same, if anything I think it is more than it was two months ago, but it is not enough for him, though he enjoys what there is of it very much. Between the nursings, he gets cream and oatmeal, which seems to agree with him pretty well. The oatmeal is of course the gruel, strained, and the cream is the Highland Evaporated. I find it always a little acid and have to put soda in it to counteract. I have no doubt if Sherwood could only have some of the nice milk and cream from his grandfather's farm, he would thrive finely, but there is no reliable milk to be obtained here, it would not be safe to give any of it unboiled,

---

[119] A Korean chamber pot.
[120] Four times a day.

and if it were boiled it would be so constipating for him. Then it costs 30 cents per quart water and all. Sherwood is growing up to be quite a good looking baby, but then I suppose I am not a good judge for to tell the truth he begins to look to me just like Sherwood Hall, and I can't compare him with other babies as though he were someone else. I see now how it would be hard for a mother to know if her child was homely, and how easy it would be to get used to any peculiarity, and not see what other people are unable to overlook. I suppose it is well it is so. I am anxious to hear what Sherwood's Papa will say, for when he first sees him, and for a day or two it will be much the same as if he was someone else's child I would think. It has been so long, in fact more than half of Sherwood's life, and he has changed so much in that time.

I expect Doctor home in seven more days. Oh, how glad we shall be. In his letters he says, "Dr. Scranton and I have had very pleasant times together, I don't expect we will have any further trouble. It is a great thing to know each other, and this has been accomplished during our two weeks together here." Doctor says nothing about the building which was to have gone up so soon, and be furnished at once, but I overheard Mrs. Dr. Scranton tell Mr. Hulbert that Dr. Scranton wrote that all idea of building at Pyong Yang must be given up for the present; so I take it that Dr. Scranton sees the work now as it really is in that difficult field, and not as it looks in fancy and theory from his chair in his pleasant study here in Söul.

I am plodding away at the first quarter of the second year's course. Our examination will come now as soon as

Diary of Dr. Rosetta Hall 1892-1894

Dr. Hall gets back I expect. I have been able to get over from ten to fifteen pages nearly every day in the grammar, will finish it this week I think, and then can have next week to finish reading *The Two Friends* and for review. I shall be so thankful if I can feel quite well prepared, for one time there, when Sherwood required so much attention, I feared I should have to give up the study of the language altogether. However, I suppose I have done it somewhat at his expense. At least if I could have spent one of the three or four hours spent in study each day out of doors, I have no doubt I should have had more milk. But then, he has continued to improve, if he had not I would have given it out. I think next time I shall take two quarters to do one quarter's work, and fall behind so that Doctor and I can study together. (We are three quarters apart.) It would be so much easier and pleasanter. If he had been home this winter, he had expected to take two quarters' work in one quarter, but I am afraid he will not be able to do it now. If he could have done that we would have been together very soon. I am housekeeper this month also.

> "The trivial round, the common task,
> will furnish all we ought to ask:
> room to deny ourselves; a road
> to bring us daily nearer God."[121]

I have good letters from the home folks—have received a letter from Mother, from Frank[122], from Maggie and from

---

[121] John Keble.
[122] Rev. Frank R. Sherwood is Rosetta's brother.

Diary of Dr. Rosetta Hall 1892-1894

Uncle Robert[123] since they learned of Sherwood's birth. Joe sent a US dollar to Sherwood. Mother writes that I was a very much like Sherwood in being so constipated when a baby, though I did not suffer so much pain, and was able to have my stool without an enema if mother removed my diaper and held me out over the chamber. She says I saved her much work that way, that when I was 3 weeks old she went home with me to her father's and staid a week; and I never soiled a diaper while I was there. She used to give me magnesia etc. but nothing seemed to amount to much until I got big enough to eat other food beside milk. Strange how Sherwood should have inherited with intensification my baby habit. It seems my last article was printed in the New York Witness.[124] Mother writes,

> "Pa took the Witness to read yesterday, and he says 'Well, well,' then he read aloud the first notice in the Editorial, 'Be sure you read Dr. Rosetta Sherwood Hall's letter from Korea. It illustrates very forcibly the necessity for medical missions among uncivilized races.' Then Pa says, 'That's what makes us proud.' (He said 'me' but I said 'us') The letter is about the little boy you doctored and the Korean doctor too. Didn't you cry to see the little boy treated so? The first time I read it I couldn't help but to shed tears."

This altogether sounded so quaint and comical to me that I thought I'd put it down just as Mother wrote it. Maggie writes, "Your husband's postal reached home safely, and

---

[123] Uncle Robert Gildersleeve is Rosetta's mother's brother.
[124] New York Weekly Witness.

Diary of Dr. Rosetta Hall 1892-1894

we were very much surprised and pleased. It does not seem possible that you have a dear little baby born away out in that heathen land." Frank says, "You gave us quite a surprise—did not think of you going into the family business. The boy will scarcely know his nationality. Kiss him for us. The darling little Sherwood, suppose he will be a missionary certain."

Saturday, March 17—I was expecting the Doctor home today, and he may come yet, but I have just received letters from him written the 8th and 9th in which he says Chang Sikey and family had not arrived yet. They left here February 28, and Yousanie went with them, and I expected surely they'd get there by March 8th. Doctor writes he is making arrangements to return as soon as Chang Sikey and family arrive, and he can get them settled. Chang Sikey was formerly Mr. Ohlinger's cook, and he is a very earnest Christian, one of the very few Koreans who seems to really have his heart converted. Doctor has been employing him as his Helper ever since Mr. Ohlinger left, and now he has had him move his family to Pyong Yang. Doctor seems quite encouraged with the work there. There were several that were going to be baptized last Sunday. Doctor says they have to endure a great deal of prosecution, but it is doing them good. He has also started a school[125], has an earnest Christian teacher, and 13 boys already. They study

---

[125] William James Hall started to teach students since early 1894 and this school became Gwang-Sung Boys' School. The Gwang-Sung High School website records the founding date to be April 6, 1894, but according to Rosetta's diary, the school was already started on March 17, 1894.

the catechism mornings and nights, and *Enmun*[126] and Chinese the rest of the day. Doctor says,

> "The light is beginning to dawn here for which I praise God. We will trust Him and push forward. I am learning to trust Him more. It is so good to rest fully in Him. How many times He has to teach me those lessons. How patient and loving He is with me."

> "Well, my darling, I am expecting a good letter when Chang Sikey arrives, perhaps he will be here today. My heart leaps for joy at the thought of so soon being with you again. I was just thinking this morning that one day with you was better than a thousand without you. I never realized so fully before how much I love you, my precious darling."

4 p.m., more letters came from the Doctor, but they are older than what I received this morning, bearing dates of February 26, 28, and March 3 and 6th. In them he speaks as if he would not be home until a week from today, and perhaps later. Oh, I hope it may not be so, and yet it is all right if work needs him. Jesus will help me to be patient and brave yet another week. As Doctor says in his letter "we will make every trial a steppingstone lifting us near to God." February 26th, Doctor says,

> "You know how I long to be with you. Sometimes the longing is so great it is almost unbearable and I go to God for grace. Oh, my precious one, I am so

---

[126] Korean script.

Diary of Dr. Rosetta Hall 1892-1894

glad you are mine. I don't know how I could live without you.

The 28th he writes,

> "This trip has been a great blessing to me in every way. It has taught me more fully to give up to God the dear ones that I love with all my heart. It cost me a great struggle to leave you so long my darling, but I believe the blessings that will follow will be worth a thousand fold. It seems to me I love you a thousand times more than ever before. Trials do me good. I need them. But I thank God He lifts me above them and enables me to rejoice continually in Him."

> "I have six men that I think are coming out strongly for Christ. They have to endure a great deal of persecution, but they are faithful in study and in attending the meetings. I am so glad to see the people here accepting Jesus as their Saviour. I have a meeting for boys every night before the regular service, about fifteen usually come and are very attentive. I questioned them last night upon what I had taught them before, and was surprised to see how much they had learned. I am giving every morning to study and every afternoon to seeing patients and exercise, and the evenings to meetings. I treated 16 patients today, and three of these were out-calls. Everything is going on smoothly and I am daily making friends and winning the confidence of the Koreans. I think we are in Pyong Yang to stay now."

Doctor is living on food procured in Pyong Yang mostly, and prepared by a Pyong Yang boy that Chang Sikey

Diary of Dr. Rosetta Hall 1892-1894

trained a little before he left. His bill of fare is "*Chang Kook Pop*,"[127] whatever that is, for breakfast, pheasant, *kimchi*, and soup for dinner, pancakes and honey for supper. He says, "You know I never cared much for a variety, and the three meals being different gives me all the variety I desire. I have not suffered with indigestion at all. The food is very nutritious and agrees with me."

My poor dear darling brave Doctor, how I long to be with him, and help take care of him. He doesn't know how to take care of himself, but always neglects himself for others. Oh, I hope nothing will prevent my returning with him. He says in one place,

> "Things were in such an unsettled state here for a time, we did not know what the governor or people would do with our being here, that it seemed to unwise to lay any plans, and then I wanted to talk everything over with you, but it seems to me now there will be no difficulty in your coming up as we had planned. Dr. Scranton likes the property very much. He was very comfortable here. We had good times together, not one particle of friction, neither do I think there will be any more.

Doctor says,

> "I am glad our darling boy is getting along so well. I long to see him. I rejoice the time is getting near when I shall be with you again, my precious ones. If it were not that I am doing this for Jesus I don't know how I could endure being away from you. I

---

[127] Rice-beef-vegetable soup.

prize your precious love more than anything else in this world. It is a mine of wealth that gets richer and richer; and I am sure will continue to do so throughout our lives. Well, darling, I guess you will think I write nothing but love-letters, but I must give vent to these small expressions of the great love that is in my heart for you."

Am I not blessed above women with such a precious lover for my husband? I didn't mean to write quite so much, but then Doctor's letters are written in lead pencil, and I do want to keep some of the things he has written, not that they are any better than what he has often spoken, but I can't remember the spoken words long enough to write them just as he says them, and these I can copy and then they are preserved, and easier to refer to than the letters anyhow; I am adopting that plan more and more I notice. I used to try to keep all my letters, but they grow too cumbersome, and I find I seldom look at them after a few weeks; but my journal is so easy to pick up and read in an odd moment now and then, and I often enjoy over again in this way the previous words of husband, mother, brother, sister or friend.

It is now 6 p.m., and Doctor has not yet arrived, and I must fear he may not, for another week. Well, I must abide by my text. "Your Heavenly Father knoweth what things ye have need of."[128] If it is best, I know He will bring back my dear husband safely to me tonight.

He came 10 p.m.

---

[128] Matthew 6:8.

Diary of Dr. Rosetta Hall 1892-1894

Monday, April 2, 1894

Ye are my witnesses, saith the LORD, and my servant whom I have chosen. Isa. 43:10

> If you went to serve your race, go where no one else will go, and do what no one else will do. —Mary Lyon

A very happy day. I have consent of Superintendent at last to accompany my husband to Pyong Yang upon his next trip.

Of course about that first thing after Doctor came home I asked if he still thought it would be all right for me to accompany him on his return trip, and to my surprise and great disappointment (as he had written in one of his letters it would) he said no. I wanted to know why, and he told me of several pretty bad experiences he had with the people there, and then that there was not a good fence or gate-house to our property and no room where he could to see the men etc. and so on. I listened and for a day or two I thought Doctor really felt I better not go, but little by little as I put one thing together with another it came to me that it was not my Doctor that thought this, but Dr. Scranton. He had told Dr. Cutler last winter that if Doctor did not build he could not let him take me to Pyong Yang.

So one day I just faced Doctor with it, and said, "Of course I know it will be very very difficult for me to go to Pyong Yang and live under the circumstances, but I doubt if it be any worse than many have encountered in opening up new work in the interior of China, and I believe as far as you are concerned you'd let me go, but Dr. Scranton will not give his consent, and you do not want me to know this for fear I will kick, is not this so?" And after a time I made him own it up. As soon as I found it was only Dr. Scranton "consent" that lay between, I at once set to work to get it. Of course it would be natural for me to just say I would go to the place my husband was sent consent or not consent, but I knew this would displease Doctor very much, and would probably not be best, at least if the consent might be obtained, and I had faith to believe it would. Fortunately for me, I knew Mrs. M. F. Scranton was in favor of my going for she is very anxious to have woman's work opened up in Pyong Yang and unfortunately again for me, she herself took it into her head to make a country trip before her son's return, and she was so pleased with it, even with the many difficulties, that I felt she would not think them so great for me, so one day when Doctor and I called there to see Mrs. Isabella Bird Bishop while Doctor and this lady were busy engaged in talking, I asked Mrs. M. F. Scranton what she thought about my going back with the Doctor, and I found out that she thought it would be all right and likely no harder than it was for Mrs. Dr. Scranton when they first came to Söul as she had one sick baby and was carrying another, and everything was new and strange and she had to live in the native house and stand a great deal of "*kukyong*[129]'ing" etc. I also found that Mrs. Scranton evidently did not know that her son's consent was the only thing that prevented my going, but that she thought Doctor was afraid to have me and his baby go. Today, as Dr. Scran-

---

[129] Sightseeing.

ton returned a few days ago, time enough for his mother to have expressed her ideas to him, I asked Doctor to go and talk to him again about my going; and if he wouldn't give his consent I would go myself to him, and then if he didn't I should take it as the Lord's will that I should not go, and would be content. So Doctor went, and I knelt in prayer and asked God to bless the two doctors and help them to come to the right conclusion, that it was His will and not my own I wanted. I dared not ask for my own. I would not have it if I might.

> "Which is the true, safe way?
> Which would be in vain?
>
> I am not wise to know,
> Not sure of foot to go,
> My blind eyes cannot see
> What is so clear to Thee;
> Lord, make it clear to me.
>
> Being perplexed, I say,
> Lord, make it right!
> Night is as day to Thee,
> Darkness as light.
>
> I am afraid to touch
> Things that involve so much;
> My trembling hand may shake,
> My skill-less hand may break."[130]

---

[130] From "My Prayer" by an anonymous author.

Diary of Dr. Rosetta Hall 1892-1894

It only seems to me that it would be so much more satisfactory all around if I could make one trip to Pyong Yang before next Annual Meeting, so that we may know more how the people and the officials are going to take our living there, and so that if all goes well we may make calculations accordingly at Annual Meeting. Otherwise, we may think that all things right, and move up there at quite an expense, only to have to return, and work be put back longer than if we went only with the intention of staying a short time. Then too, it will be much easier for Esther and Sylvia and for their folks to let them go this first time if they can expect them back again soon. And it is so hard for Doctor and I to be separated so much and to live along this way not knowing whether we can ever hope to work together in Pyong Yang before it is made an open port or not. Everything seems to be as ripe now for the trial as any time can be. Mr. Moffett thinks it all right. Both Boards[131] at home are looking forward and expecting it with interest. Dr. Scranton had just gotten a letter to that effect, and he gave his consent without much hesitation. He said he certainly thought it would be the best thing to open up the work. I always got along well with Korean people and they loved me, but he thought it would be very unpleasant for me, and wondered that I'd want go, until things could be fixed up more comfortable.

---

[131] The Board of Foreign Missions of the Methodist Episcopal Church and of the Woman's Foreign Missionary Society (W.F.M.S.).

Diary of Dr. Rosetta Hall 1892-1894

It seems that Dr. Scranton at the time he made that trouble for Dr. Hall last winter was not satisfied without writing to Dr. Leonard, and just as we were packing up for Pyong Yang, Doctor received this encouraging letter from Dr. Leonard. I pin it here with a copy of Doctor's reply.[132]

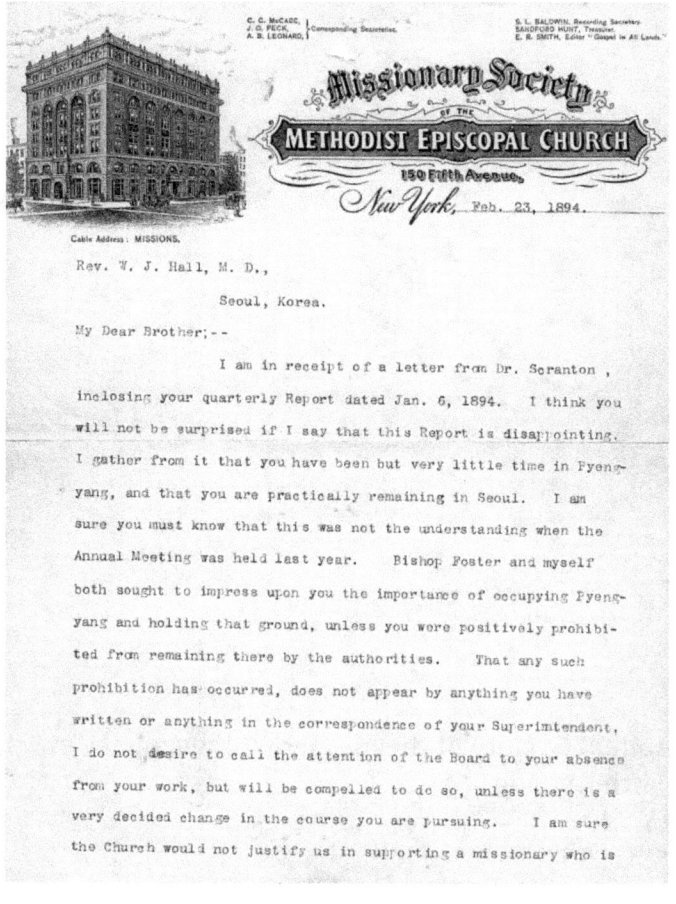

---

[132] Rosetta has saved clips of Dr. Leonard's articles, including the following on *The Christian Advocate*, which states, "He further noted the fact, that in the twenty-four years of his official life, Dr. Leonard took great pride that he had never used a harsh word in a letter to any missionary, ..."

Diary of Dr. Rosetta Hall 1892-1894

W. J. H. --- 2

not doing the work to which he has been appointed. I am speaking to you in plain words, but in all kindness. The difficulties to which you refer do not seem to be of such a character as to justify you in remaining absent from your appointment. Of course there will be hardships, but they must be endured. This is understood when a missionary enters a foreign field.

I learn from the Supt. that you carried your case to the British Consul and that he gave his influence against the erection of the house that had been planned for you in Pyeng-yang. So far as I can see, there was no necessity for your revealing the plans of the Mission to the British Consul. It would have been time enough for you to have appealed to him when your safety was really in danger. The Presbyterians seem to have no difficulty in occupying Pyeng-yang, and certainly Methodist missionaries should be as industrious and heroic as any to be found in Korea. Perhaps before this reaches its destination, you will be in Pyeng-yang, and I hope you will remain there, (unless ordered by the authorities to leave) until the ensuing Annual Meeting of the Mission.

With kindest regards to Mrs. Hall, believe me to be

Yours sincerely,

A. B. Leonard

Fairly well taken back in Dr. Leonard's letter Feb. 23/95 which are

Missionary Society of the Methodist Episcopal Church
150 Fifth Avenue
New York
Feb. 23, 1894

Rev. W. J. Hall, M.D.
Seoul, Korea
My Dear Brother; --

Diary of Dr. Rosetta Hall 1892-1894

I am in receipt of a letter from Dr. Scranton, inclosing your quarterly Report dated Jan. 6, 1894. I think you will not be surprised if I say that this Report is disappointing. I gather from it that you have been but very little time in Pyeng-yang, and that you are practically remaining in Seoul. I am sure you must know that this was not the understanding when the Annual Meeting was held last year. Bishop Foster and myself both sought to impress upon you the importance of occupying Pyeng-yang and holding that ground, unless you were positively prohibited from remaining there by the authorities. That any such prohibition has occurred, does not appear by anything you have a written or anything in the correspondence of your Superintendent. I do not desire to call the attention of the Board to your absence from your work, but will be compelled to do so, unless there is a very decided change in the course you are pursuing. I am sure the Church would not justify us in supporting a missionary who is not doing the work to which he has been appointed. I am speaking to you in plain words, but in all kindness. The difficulties to which you refer do not seem to be of such a character as to justify you in remaining absent from your appointment. Of course there will be hardships, but they must be endured. This is understood when a missionary enters a foreign field.

I learned from the Superintendent that you carried your case to the British Consul and that he gave his influence against the erection of the house that had been planned for you in Pyeng-yang. So far as I can see, there was no necessity for your revealing the plans of the Mission to the British Consul. It would have been time enough for you to have appealed to him when your safety was really in danger. The Presbyterians seem to have no difficulty in occupying Pyeng-yang, and certainly Methodist missionaries should be as industrious and heroic as any to be found in Korea. Perhaps before this reaches its destination, you will be in Pyeng-yang, and I hope you will remain there, (unless ordered by the authorities to leave) until the ensuing Annual Meeting of the Mission.

With kindest regards to Mrs. Hall, believe me to be

Yours sincerely,

A. B. Leonard

Diary of Dr. Rosetta Hall 1892-1894

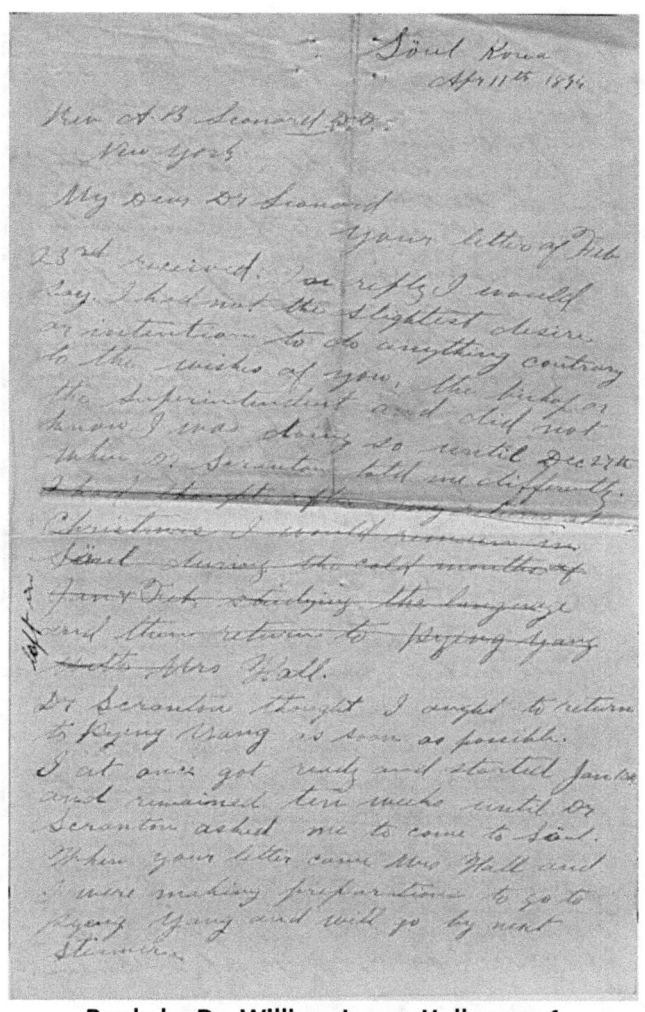

Reply by Dr. William James Hall, page 1

On my first trip last fall I was unable to get into either one of our houses as the men who occupied them had been forbidden by the governor to let a foreigner stay in the houses and I did not think it wise to force an entrance. After remaining there for a few days I had an opportunity of coming down to Seoul by steamer and came only for the purpose of finding out ways and means of going and coming by steamer and as they run very irregularly I did not know when I would have another opportunity.

During my stay in Seoul I spent the time in faithful study of the language. I did not think anyone would criticise my being here during my wife's sickness.

I returned to Pyeng Yang twenty days after Mrs. Hall's confinement and stayed until Christmas.

In regard to the house that was planned for Pyeng Yang. I did not think it wise at this stage of our work in Pyeng Yang to build a house.

Reply by Dr. William James Hall, page 2

Diary of Dr. Rosetta Hall 1892-1894

Söul, Korea
April 11, 1894

Rev. A. B. Leonard, D.D.
New York

My dear Dr. Leonard,

Your letter of Feb. 23 received. In reply I would say I had not the slightest desire or intention to do anything contrary to the wishes of you, the Bishop or the Superintendant and did not know I was doing so until Dec. 27th when Dr. Scranton told me differently. I had thought after my return at Christmas I would remain in Söul during the cold months of Jan. and Feb. studying the language and then return to Pyong Yang with Mrs. Hall.

Dr. Scranton thought I ought to return to Pyong Yang as soon as possible. I at once got ready and started Jan. 10th and remained ten weeks until Dr. Scranton asked me to come to Söul. When your letter came, Mrs. Hall and I were making preparations to go to Pyong Yang and will go by next steamer.

On my first trip last fall, I was unable to get into either one of our houses as the men who occupied them had been forbidden by the governor to let a foreigner step in the houses and I did not think it wise to force an entrance. After remaining there for a few days, I had an opportunity of coming down to Söul by steamer and came only for the purpose of finding out ways and means of going and coming by steamer and as they run very irregularly I did not know when I would have another opportunity.

Diary of Dr. Rosetta Hall 1892-1894

During my stay in Sŏul, I spent the time in faithful study of the language. I did not think anyone would criticize my being here during my wife's sickness. I returned to Pyong Yang twenty days after Mrs. Hall's confinement and stayed until Christmas.

In regard to the house that was planned for Pyong Yang, I did not think it wise at this stage of our work in Pyong Yang to build a house. But I was willing to go ahead and build if our Consul did not block my way. I did not know then that Dr. Scranton intended going north so soon or I would not have mentioned the subject to the Consul. The Consul had promised to help me in getting into our houses and holding our property in Pyong Yang and I did not know I was doing wrong in speaking to him about building there. I felt quite positive if Dr. Scranton fully understood how we were situated he would not think it best to build.

After Dr. Scranton visited Pyong Yang, he told me, "I would not advise building a house here at present as it is all you can do to hold what you have got." Dr. Scranton and I spent two very pleasant weeks together in Pyong Yang.

The difficulty has arisen through a misunderstanding of my report and probably from my failure to properly represent the conditions existing in P. Y. as bearing upon the removal of myself and family. I had purposed to move there at as an early date as possible but account of Mrs. Hall's condition and other difficulty in getting into our houses, I thought it would frustrate all our plans to move in sooner than our doing.

Diary of Dr. Rosetta Hall 1892-1894

Dr. Scranton told me since your letter came he was very sorry for causing me this trouble. He will no doubt fully report to you the state of the work at P.Y.

The Presbyterians are in a much less trouble [letter ends here][133]

---

[133] The rest of the letter reads: "The Presbyterians are in a much less hostile district in we are in. You remember they were in Pyong Yang when the trouble occurred a year ago when the governor ordered those who had sold the houses to our men to give back the money and receive back the deeds. The Presbyterians were there and gave up their property. I was in Euiju at that time and had the deeds with me. I thought it best to hold onto the property if possible. The Presbyterians have bought again in a district that is quite friendly and is well adapted to the work but will not be suitable to live in in the summer time. They took possession of their house immediately after buying it and there is never any difficulty to get the former owners to move out at that time. But on account of the order of the governor the former owners of our houses went back in the houses again and after they had spent the money they had received for the houses there was a great deal more difficulty to get them to give up the houses and this has made us some enemies. We are trying to meet the difficulties as best as we can and are trusting the Lord to clear the way. I am glad you and Bishop Foster reached home safely. Yours sincerely, W. J. Hall" **Missionary Files: Methodist Episcopal Church; Missionary Correspondence, 1846-1912, Microfilm S3458, Reel 16, No. 0529.**

Diary of Dr. Rosetta Hall 1892-1894

But I was willing to go ahead and build if our consul did not block my way. I did not know then that Dr. Scranton intended going north so soon or I would not have mentioned the subject to the consul. The consul had promised to help me in getting into our houses and holding our property in Pyeng Yang and I did not know I was wrong in speaking to him about building there.

I felt quite positive if Dr. Scranton fully understood how we were situated he would not think it best to build.

After Dr. Scranton visited Pyeng Yang he told me "I would not advise building a house here at present as it is all you can do to hold what you have got."

Dr. Scranton and I spent two very pleasant weeks together in Pyeng Yang. The difficulty has arisen through a misunderstanding of my report and probably from my failure to properly represent the conditions existing in pg 2 as bearing upon the removal of myself & family. I had purposed to move there at as early date as possible

Reply by Dr. William James Hall, page 3

Diary of Dr. Rosetta Hall 1892-1894

Reply by Dr. William James Hall, page 4

Thursday, May 10, 1894, Pyong Yang[134]

For, when we were come into Macedonia, our flesh had no rest, but we were troubled on every side; without were fightings, within were fears. Never-

---

[134] William James Hall's mission report about this visit was published in *Chinese Recorder*, September 1894 (Appendix 7).

Diary of Dr. Rosetta Hall 1892-1894

theless God, that comforteth those that are cast down, comforted us. II Cor. 7:5,6

"In the midst of the mighty city,
    And the trampling of many feet,
In the midst of the looks of strangers,
    Crowding the busy street,
There comes the sound of a whisper
    To the listening gladdened ear
And Thy children, Lord are not fearful
    For they know that Thou art near."[135]

This is Sherwood's 6 months birthday. How he has grown this last month. You would scarcely recognize him as the same baby that left Söul three weeks ago. We spent two weeks in Chemulpo waiting for the steamer, and then we had a typhoon on the way and had to anchor for over a day and a half, so we were from Friday noon until Tuesday noon upon the saltwater coming here. Everyone else was very seasick the most of the time, but Sherwood thought all the rocking and rolling was for his amusement and he was so good, and slept so well and ate so much. He is as rosy and plump now as one could wish to see. He is so good-natured and has really developed into a good-looking baby in the eyes of other people as well as of his fond parents. He is 26½ inches long and circumference of head is 17 inches. I have not weighed him in a month, then he only weighed 13½ pounds, but I am sure he must weigh 16 now; but I have no way to weigh him. He is just beginning to learn to kiss, and he is a real little lover. He got his first fall

---

[135] Robert Rutter Jenkins.

Diary of Dr. Rosetta Hall 1892-1894

yesterday, rolled off of a box 2 feet high with a quilt over where I laid him down to take a nap. I heard the fall and found him lying on his face; of course, he cried pretty lustily but he soon stopped when mother comforted his little frightened heart. He is cutting two teeth.

We came up here from the river Tuesday in closed chairs, got here about 2 p.m. I had some charming glimpses in our grounds of blooming fruit trees and yellow roses, but have not been able to go out and take a look around on account of the *kukyong* people both men and women. Doctor told those that came and asked that I would see the women in sets of ten each five minutes at a time in my room tomorrow afternoon. In that way I could get through with 120 an hour and they'd all have a fair chance. All seemed pleased with the idea and we had no trouble in sending them away that day nor forenoon of yesterday. We set to work and got our two little rooms cleaned, one of which I have mine and the baby's bed, my trunk, a box and one chair with a few shelves that do as dressing bureau for the present. In the other is our table, my steamer chair, and the two chairs Doctor brought up before. We swept the walls all down and bought new matting for the floors and I adorned the walls with a few pictures. Doctor will put his cot up in this room every night and take it down in the morning for the present. After a time, we will have one more room to use which will be our dining and sitting room. The Kims, the former owners of this house are in there now. Yousanie had the large Korean kitchen cleaned and we have put up the little cook-stove and put in our boiler like a Korean Kettle, and two rice kettles for our Koreans; and though we are not all unpacked yet we already feel quite at home, as I wrote to Mrs. M. F. Scranton last night, "Perhaps you can imagine how happy I am and with what a sense of satisfaction I write "Pyong Yang" at the head of my letter."

Right after tiffin, I began seeing the women, after carefully locking up everything that might easily be carried off. Three sets of ten came in and went out on time very orderly and many of those waiting in the packed court and outside the gate wished to continue the order but later arrivals who didn't well understand would push in and soon the two rooms were packed so full that none could stir and the only way to get them to go out seemed for me to go myself upon the *marrow*[136] and let them see by the court yard full. This I did, and saw the court yard packed full four different times probably at least 1500 women and children. And then we had to stop their coming with the promise of seeing more today. Sherwood proved the great attraction.

At about 4 p.m., Doctor started to go to the magistrate to ask for a "*kuisyu*" to guard us on account of so many *kukyong* people in our walls and gates not being in a condition to keep order. Upon his way a messenger from the Governor met him and asked to see his passport etc. The Governor did not see him himself, said he was very busy, but had an under official see him. He asked Doctor about the houses. The Doctor said they were bought by Mr. You, and he gave us permission to stop in them while we were

---

[136] *maru* is planked porch which connects inside and outside of Korean house.

here, that we could not stop in an inn as it was too small to see patients in. He wanted to know why I came, Doctor said that I was also a doctor and came to see the sick women and children and that we were to return to Söul after a little while. Kim, a young man in employ of the Governor and one for whom Doctor got a broken watch fixed and brought him without charge from Söul to show that he meant to be his friend, this young man, the son of the Captain of this district, spoke up before the Doctor and said to under official that if they allowed me to stay here, one foreigner after another with come till Pyong Yang would all be taken by foreigners.

The official said he thought the Governor would see Doctor in the morning. We had supper, prayers, and went to bed in peace and happiness to be awakened at 2 a.m. by two of the Pyong Yang Christians, Mr. O and Mr. Ni coming to tell us that faithful Chang Sikey who has been living and teaching here ever since Doctor returned to Söul was cast into prison, also Kim the former owner of this house, and the former owner of Mr. Moffett's house, and Han, Mr. Moffett's preacher were also in prison. It seems about 1 a.m., someone knocked at Chang Sikey's window and said he was sent by Dr. Hall. So Chang Sikey opened the door and he was taken by servants of the Captain of this district, and beaten and put into stocks and was suffering very much. They said they would beat him again this morning. A little later Chang Sikey's wife came. They said they did not dare beat Dr. Hall, so they took Chang Sikey in his stead. At 6:30 o'clock, Doctor went to ask to see the Governor. He waited till 7:30 and they said the Governor was sleeping and

Diary of Dr. Rosetta Hall 1892-1894

couldn't see him. So he telegraphed at once to Söul to Dr. Scranton ([This part about the telegraph] should come after O's arrest):

> "Chang Sikey stocks, O, Moffett's Han beaten, former owner of tree house all now prison, ask protection family and servants."

While Doctor was gone they sent word if we would give 100,000 cash it would save Chang Sikey from a beating this morning. I did not have that much in the house, but told a man to go and tell Doctor. Doctor returned about 8 o'clock. He had been to the prison and saw them all. Chang Sikey was suffering very much, the stocks being very tightly screwed on. Mr. O had accompanied Doctor, and just while the Doctor was in the house a few moments, he was grabbed right in front of our ground and also carried to prison and put in with the others in the room for thieves. Doctor then started out again after eating his breakfast (sent above telegram to Söul) to demand an interview with the Governor. The English interpreter in the Chinese telegraph office has always been a friend to Dr. Hall and Doctor asked him as a favor if he would not accompany him to see the Governor and he very kindly consented to do so. Doctor was gone this time from 11 a.m. to 2 p.m. *Kukyong* women and children kept coming in groups of tens and twelves all day. They were very orderly, the most of them cleanly dressed and very good faced people. I am sure I shall like the women of the Pyong Yang very much. They scarcely noticed anything about the house, but spent all their time on the baby or me. They all called Sherwood "lovely" and most of them thought I was too. I asked them

Diary of Dr. Rosetta Hall 1892-1894

if they were not afraid to come in this house as our friends, several of them, had been cast into prison today; but they did not seem to be afraid. I had quite nice talks with them, found that I could make them understand me well, and I understood them easily. It was of course very tiresome for me with the strain of the great disturbance all the time and our Korean helpers frightened, to keep a cheerful face and manner, but I did it. During this time, poor Chang Sikey came to this house under guard of his jailers, and they again demanded the 100,000 cash to save him from another beating. Later Mr. O came in the same way; he seemed very cheerful and said it was all right, he thought they would soon receive orders for their release. He didn't want me to give the money. I think poor Chang Sikey did, but then he had been in prison much longer than Mr. O and had those terrible stocks pinching him, and it was enough to make his courage fail. About 1p.m., a servant of the magistrate came and asked to see me and gave me a paper written in Chinese. Esther said that they said we must get out of the house, so supposing it might be an order to that effect I said I could not read it, and refused to receive it. They then posted it on the gate, and a friend of Doctor's afterward interpreted it as something like this. It was written by the magistrate next to the Governor to Captain Kim of this district, and said that

> "He must make the former owner of this house to get it back. He had thus been ordered a long time ago. Dr. Hall had now come with his wife which was a sign that he would live long here, therefore right away the former owner must take the house back. Many *kukyong* people make great disturbance,

> therefore let only patients come, other people to tie up. No one must listen to preaching as both Catholicism and Protestantism were very bad."

It had three official stamps upon it—from what afterward occurred I do not know whether they gave it to me by mistake or whether the Captain after reading it, sent it to scare us.

> At 2 p.m., Doctor returned saying this telegram had come from Dr. Scranton.

> "Legations will act at once. Telegraph particulars of difficulty."

And he had telegraphed,

> "All that can be found that have had anything to do with Moffett or Self in prison. No reason given. Suffering intense agony, relief needed immediately. Governor refuses to see me, listen to appeals or give protection. We are ordered out of house."

Doctor again hastened off. Governor still refused to see him, even though the Chinese interpreter told him he had telegraphed to Söul and would do so again.

> At 4 p.m., Doctor again returned with telegram from Consul General Gardener[137] saying,

---

[137] C.T. Gardner, acting British Consul General in Korea until September 1894, while Mr. Walter C. Hillier was on leave.

Diary of Dr. Rosetta Hall 1892-1894

"Will require foreign office to telegraph officials to release Corean servants and so forth at once and afford you and family adequate protection."

At this time, servants came from the jail again demanding money or all would again be beaten, also a servant from Captain Kim demanding the papers stuck upon our gate. Doctor had just previously secured it; and we all thought it best to keep it, though we did not know at that time that it was addressed to Captain Kim. Doctor was about ready to eat when they first asked for it; so we told them to wait, and later he told them to come in the morning he was too tired to see them now—thought he would come Korean fashion over them. But they plead so much he finally went out, and they explained how they would be beaten if they went back to Captain Kim without that paper; he had been commanded by the magistrate to secure it. I told Doctor not to give it—that of course the Captain would tell them that, that they might use every means to secure it. Finally they went off. They had not much more than gone before I heard such a noise like a mad bull bellowing and pawing the ground in the rage. It proved to be the Captain himself, the one that had Mr. No, Doctor's Helper, whipped the last time he was up here. Mr. No said he was no man, he was a pig, and I believe if he is no worse than that he must at least be one of those pigs that devils entered into. Doctor went out and tried to reason with him, but he would listen to nothing, went on blowing in the greatest rage I ever saw a man in. Little Sherwood had just gotten soundly asleep, and the noise made him wide awake in a few moments. Yousanie happened to be out in the court. He had kept pretty close all day, and I only wish he might have been in then, Captain Kim had him pointed out to him as one of Doctor's servants and he immediately set upon him, seized him by the top-knot and beat and kicked him in white fury and ordered to be carried off. Doctor knew it was only to get hold of this paper, but he could not withstand the appeals of Yousanie to give it up under such a circumstances, then the Satanic man went off satisfied.

8 p.m., Minister Sill's[138] telegram came. It said,

> "British Consul General and I have insisted that foreign office order the immediate release of Moffett's and your employees, and facts and reasons laid before us together with your protection according to treaty."

At the same time came a kind telegram from Mr. Moffett saying,

> "Joshua one nine, tell neighbors contents of telegrams."

Joshua 1:9 reads,

> "Have not I commanded thee? Be strong and of good courage; be not afraid, neither be discouraged for the Lord thy God is with thee whithersoever thou goest."

We had prayer, and retired at 10 p.m. My bed crosses in front of a small paper covered window at the back of the

---

[138] John M. B. Sill, Unites States Minister to Korea from February 1894 to April 1897.

Diary of Dr. Rosetta Hall 1892-1894

room. Doctor had opened it to letting some fresh air. It was covered with a thin lawn curtain and I forgot it was open and stood in front of it undressing, when suddenly came a stone hurled evidently by someone who saw me standing there as there was a light in my room. It struck an earthen jar, breaking it just in front of the window. It made such a crash just like breaking a glass window that it quite startled us all. I ran into Doctor's room and told Sylvia to bring the baby quickly, not knowing how many more would follow. Doctor got up and closed the window, and as no more seemed to be coming, I went to bed, taking the precaution, however, of placing my thick comfortable between me and the window. We all had refreshing sleep.

> "All weary thought and care
>   Lord, we resign;
> Ours is to do, to bear
>   To choose is Thine."[139]

Friday, May 11, 1894, 7 a.m.

Servant of the Governor (son of Captain Kim) came and said the telegram to the Governor had come (as we expected) but he said the message was that the British and American Minister had seen the King and had agreed that Pyong Yang was no place in which to preach the Gospel, that the King said Dr. Hall was a bad man, and ordered the Governor to behead all Christians today. Of course we think it must be a lie, but then they have changed Chang

---

[139] Anonymous poem titled "Thy Will be Done" in Hymns from the Land of Luther.

Diary of Dr. Rosetta Hall 1892-1894

Sikey from the cell of thieves to the death cell, and have put him in stocks again, and I don't understand that. Doctor went to see him, and he himself seems to have given up in discouragement. They beat him so much and threaten him with death all the time so, that I suppose, the poor fellow dies a hundred deaths, and at this slow rate of the Governor obeying the telegram, I am afraid he will die before he gets released. Doctor cries every time he goes to see him it is so terrible. The reason he is treated so much worse than Mr. O and Mr. Han is because when they ask him to renounce the Jesus doctrine, he refuses to do so, when they ask him if he will preach anymore if he should be let out, he says he will. Praise the Lord for the Korean Paul![140]

Doctor has gone to the telegraph office again to send word of Yousani's beating in his presence, and of what the Governor's servant says the telegram to Governor said, and that instead of releasing them, they are put in death cell.

9 a.m., the Captain of the district has ordered the water man to bring us no water under penalty of a beating. As we washed for baby yesterday, there is scarcely enough to-day for his food let alone ours. All continue to say that Chang Sikey and Han will be beheaded today for having preached the Gospel. Our Koreans are all downcast and just sit down and give up in despair, bewailing their coming to Pyong

---

[140] After becoming the first ordained Korean Methodist minister, Rev. Chang-Sik Kim went everywhere in Korea evangelized people; he faced many trials but never forsaken the Lord. Missionaries at the time called him the "Korean Paul." He probably gained this nickname because of Rosetta's description in her May 14, 1894 diary.

Diary of Dr. Rosetta Hall 1892-1894

Yang. I am trying my best to keep them cheerful and trustful this morning and they soon see that.

At noon, we received the following telegram from Consul General Gardner in reply to that Doctor sent this morning.

> "Telegram was sent last night at 11 p.m. to Pyong Yang by foreign office to release all Korean servants and Christians dire situation"

Doctor again visited prison. They yet continue to beat them and threaten them with death. They now tell us that the Governor says he don't understand his telegram, and that he will telegraph back to Söul that our neighbors all tell him that we are all "Tong Hak" folks and we and our helpers are building up many houses all over Korea to help carry on that faction. Also they say he is a relative of the queen and he does not fear punishment if he does not carry out the command of the telegram. So in answer to General Gardener's telegram he sent word they had cut off our water supply, had not released prisoners, and that they said we were all "Tong Haks" (a sort of a political and religious faction that arose in the South a year ago, and threatened rebellion, and were put down by the government). Also that from every appearance they might kill Chang Sikey and Han soon if nothing further was done.

At 4 p.m., Dr. Scranton telegraphed,

> "They will not dare kill them. Foreign office has twice sent orders to release all. President of foreign

office and English Consul now together, shall see both at once. Telegraph three times daily or more."

Later another telegram came containing a copy of the order to the Governor. It asking if it has been done. If not, "other business" will follow, demands immediate release of all imprisoned and two such sent since. Moffett and McKenzie start North Friday, arrive three days. Unless Governor defies America and England you have nothing to fear."

Doctor was away at the telegraph office when news came at about 6 o'clock that the magistrate had sent for all the men to appear before him. Esther and Sylvia were very much alarmed, and said now they would surely be killed, but I told them no, I thought it was good news, and that he would now release them. And about 7 p.m. poor Chang Sikey came staggering in, he lay down on the floor, could scarcely speak, was limp and cold, and suffering extremely, said he had been stoned all the way home by order of that Captain Kim's son the servant of the Governor. I covered him up with a warm blanket, and gave him ¼ gram of morphine in a little Spts. Chloroform and tried to keep the room quiet. Doctor returned very soon, and then went to telegraph that all had been released. About 9 p.m. Chang Sikey began to feel somewhat relieved, and he ate some food, then he told us that the magistrate wanted each of the Christians to promise they would not teach the Gospel anymore if they were released. Of course poor fellows after so much delay and not knowing well the contents of the telegram, they felt the only alternative was death, and being weakened by the cruel treatment they had received,

Diary of Dr. Rosetta Hall 1892-1894

and also the thought of their helpless families, Peter-like they promised, all except Chang Sikey. He said though some might think it is a bad doctrine he knew it was good, and would live it and teach it. The magistrate commanded him to deny Jesus and to blaspheme God, he said he couldn't do it. The magistrate then told him to go, but sent no one with him and this Kim at once ordered him to be stoned and killed and boys and men pelted him all the way to our gate. Soon Mr. O also came, he had been home first; his wife is very sick—twins were born to her but a short time ago, and she was not strong and this trouble was such a great shock, it prostrated her entirely. Mr. Ni and a young man by the name of Kim, both of whom have courageously stood right by Doctor through it all, also came in and some little boys, Yousanie, Sylvia and Esther, and I and Sherwood were in my little room, and we all had a short praise meeting together. Chang Sikey himself reading Acts xvi, and leading in prayer. The dear man that he is. Doctor said he felt like kneeling at his feet. Such a faithful martyr for Jesus; it is not the privilege of many to see.

Saturday, May 19, 1894

As thy days, so shall try strength be. Deut. 38:25

"Thy days" may be a long experience
    Of much perplexity;
The light it longs for, amid clouds so dense,
    They mind may scarcely see:
Then on thy Father cast thy confidence;
    And as thy days, thy strength shall be.
—S. J. Stone

Diary of Dr. Rosetta Hall 1892-1894

Friday the 11th proved to be the dark day, since then things have not all gone smoothly, but yet no one has been injured, and all have felt comparatively safe. All day Saturday those runners of the Governor continued to threaten and insult the Christians, but Sunday and Monday it lessened. Tuesday Mr. Moffett and Mr. McKenzie arrived. They came in 8 men chairs, but said it was a mistake they could have gotten here sooner on horseback. We were very glad to welcome them, as Doctor said he had had the care of both churches upon him and he was very glad to share the responsibility. Mr. McKenzie stays night with us, and Mr. Moffett takes tiffin and supper with us. Mr. Moffett's Han went out to meet him, and as he missed him on the way, and he had not returned yet by Thursday, Mr. Moffett sent for him. He came in during Mr. Moffett's absence and no more reached the house than the Governor's servants were after him demanding more money, or he would get a beating, he gave them money. Mr. Moffett says he has had great agony of both mind and body, and will need Mr. Moffett's presence to cheer him up, so Mr. Moffett didn't come up here yesterday. He was also afraid of more trouble if he should leave the place any length of time. Mr. Moffett sent a telegram to Minister Sill, Mr. McKenzie to Gen. Gardner, and Dr. Hall to Dr. Scranton, each giving a separate description of present affairs, but neither repeating what other had said. Altogether it amounted to about this :

> Walls torn down, stoned on street, employees insulted, former owner of house not removed, no adequate protection given. Can England give it?

Diary of Dr. Rosetta Hall 1892-1894

Mr. Moffett tells us it is very fortunate that the trouble occurred with Dr. Hall and myself in the first place, for it is the U.S. policy to keep out of all religious and political trouble, and no doubt we should have at once been recalled to Söul, US Minister Sill could not give Dr. Underwood a passport to come up here, and would not give his official consent for Mr. Moffett to come. Of course we are all very much in hopes that in the end this trouble will bring religious toleration for Korea, if so it must come mostly through England's demands. She may ask instead that Pyong Yang be made an open port. We would not like that as well, because it would mean that the Chinese and Japanese would all rush in, together with all sorts of business adventures. Pyong Yang promises to prove the richest port in Korea, on account of coal mines, gold mines, farm products etc. However, if that will be the only way we may legally be allowed to live here it may be best. We are trusting God that in His own way it may all work together for the growth of His kingdom.

The idea of the three men sending the telegrams they did yesterday was that people in Söul should do all in their power to push matters with official to secure complete protection of Christian employees, and the occupation of our houses; but in addition to that it did something that had not calculated upon. It alarmed them as to our safety in staying here especially mine and baby's, and in reply Doctor got telegram from Mr. Appenzeller that Dr. Scranton would start at once to take me home, for Doctor to stick to it if possible. As I am quite comfortable and happy here, as Doctor says the most unmoved person of all

Diary of Dr. Rosetta Hall 1892-1894

through the whole trouble, it seems like quite a needless expense for Dr. S. to come upon that purpose, and besides we need him more at that end to push matter there. Also if I should leave now, nothing would please these Pyong Yang officials more; they would feel they had gained the victory then, and we were scared out. Why! I wouldn't think of such a thing as going now. Doctor spoke to me about going that dark Friday as the steamer was just about to leave and I could have made it, but I wouldn't listen to it then, and I am sure I would not like to now; so Doctor sent a telegram at once to tell him not to come, and this morning he sent another fearing they might be too anxious about me, saying I am happy and treating patients daily.

We began Tuesday seeing patients down at the other property by the gate. Doctor has one room, and I have two; one as waiting room, and one as dispensary room. Esther accompanied me; we went in our chairs. The first day we treated 10 patients, took in 500 cash. The next day, Esther had a headache and didn't go, and I treated 13 patients, taking in good cash. Yesterday, we again had 13 patients and took in 1200 cash. Of course, it is some trouble to make them observe order, and to understand that I will only see one at a time, but it grows easier, as they learn if they will only wait, each will receive the same attention. There are many people who come only for a *kukyong*, but we keep them out pretty well until all the sick are treated and then I give them all a *kukyong* at me. We have not had any religious work as yet, but I think I will begin today, after the dispensary and the *kukyong*. I fear if we tried to do

Diary of Dr. Rosetta Hall 1892-1894

anything before, at this stage, we would not get much attention.

For a week, Sherwood and I both kept pretty well. We got such a good start at Chemulpo, then we each got a diarrhea and, he vomited a great deal, and began looking so pale. Of course we knew he missed the fresh air, and his nice walks, not having been out of the house since his arrival, so on Thursday, May 24th, we resolved to spend the whole day out doors, and we left the house in charge of Mr. McKenzie. Doctor, Mr. Moffett, Sylvia, baby, and I went out to Kejah's grave—he was the founder of Korean civilization 1122 B.C.[141] and the grounds about his burial place are beautiful. On the way out, we passed through the best cultivated ground I've seen in Korea, and along very good roads that were bordered on each side with trees and altogether it reminded me more of the road passing through father's farm[142] than of anything I have seen for four years. We had our lunch out there. Sherwood had a delightful nap in the open air, and we all came home about 6 p.m. much refreshed.

However, though my headache disappeared and I felt much better every way, Sherwood's diarrhea continued. Doctor gave him his favorite pepsin and bismuth powders, and after dispensary yesterday we took him out again for a long walk. I take him in my closed chair until we get outside of the city, then I get out and walk and Chang Sikey takes Sherwood. He enjoyed it so much and was much bet-

---

[141] The Korean nation was founded by "Dangun" in 2333 BC.
[142] The Sherwood Farm had avenue of maple trees on both sides of the main road.

Diary of Dr. Rosetta Hall 1892-1894

ter last night and continues to feel better this morning. Though the diarrhea has not quite stopped yet, he doesn't vomit much however now. I think we must try and get out for an hour after dispensary each day. We all need it. Doctor's cough that he got in coming up here last winter has never yet left him, and he raises such sputum that we both fear there may be a cavity in one of his lungs. If it does not stop before we return to Söul, we shall have a very careful examination made and act accordingly to the advice of the doctors there. Oh, how we both feared some such result as this when Dr. Scranton insisted upon Doctor's coming up here in mid-winter. However, I do hope and pray it may not prove to be the case.

Thursday, June 21, 1894

> I the Lord do keep it; I will water it every moment: lest any hurt it, I will keep it night and day. Isa. 27:3
>
> "If what I wish is good,
> And suits the will divine;
> By earth and hell in vain withstood,
> I know it shall be mine."[143]

So many things have happened since I last wrote in my journal that it will be impossible to touch upon more than a few, and I don't know that I will get them in their order.

---

[143] Charles Wesley.

Diary of Dr. Rosetta Hall 1892-1894

May 23. To our surprise, Dr. Scranton arrived. Just the day before the Kims got out of the room they had been occupying, so instead of making a dining room as I had planned, we turned it over to Dr. Scranton. It seems the British Consul had written a letter to us which Dr. Scranton brought to the effect that I and baby better get away as soon as possible. I was disappointed and Dr. Scranton thought too when he saw how matters were situated that it would be better to stay, but there was the Consul's word for it for me to come back Söul or to an open port. We hoped for a time a steamer might not come until after the first of June at least, but soon we heard one had come within a week of Dr. Scranton's arrival. I wanted them to telegraph to Mr. Gardner and obtain permission for me to stay, but they thought it is not wise.

Mr. Gardner was under the impression that we had been ordered out of the house by the officials, but that was a mistake the order from the magistrate to Captain Kim was to put in the former owner of the house which he had done, but now in the meantime after telegrams came in answer to those sent by the three men in one day, Messrs Moffett, Hall, and McKenzie went together and demand an interview with this same magistrate and they said to him, we are not fools, we know the law, and the rules of our treaty with Korea as well as you do, we have not bought property in our names in Pyong Yang, it has been bought by Korean subjects who are our friends and let us stop in the houses when we come to Pyong Yang, you have the right to do with Koreans as you please and if you order the former owner of house to give back its price and the pre-

Diary of Dr. Rosetta Hall 1892-1894

sent owner to return the deeds, it will be done, but until that is done what right have you to order the former owner to live in the house? The magistrate then denied that he had so ordered. They then said if you did not tell him to go in, will you please tell him to go out, and the magistrate said he would do so, and sure enough, he did that very night, and they moved out as soon as possible.

I felt if Mr. Gardner knew this, also that I was treating women and children at the dispensary every day from 8 to 19 patients, he would not feel that my return was so necessary. However, Dr. Scranton thought best for me to carry out the orders that had been given, and Monday, May 28, I packed my trunk and got all ready to leave on a boat that evening as the steamer was said to be leaving at 4 p.m. the next day. I had had trouble with my bowels for a day or two and after my return from the dispensary that afternoon. I had frequent movements with much pain and tenesmus; however, I got my coat and hat on and the coolies had taken the baggage, when I had another movement and Doctor found it contained blood, and we knew that meant dysentery. So Dr. Scranton thought it would be by no means advisable to be on the river all night, and so I didn't go.

All thought it providential, but it turned out rather strangely after all. I was sick three days in bed, had the best of treatment, and got along nicely so that I expected to return to my work in the dispensary the following Monday, when suddenly word came that another steamer had arrived at Posan, had been sent up in haste for Pyong Yang soldiers to help quell a rebellion that had arisen in the

Diary of Dr. Rosetta Hall 1892-1894

South. So Doctor felt it his duty to take me back the first opportunity offered as Mr. Gardner had sent no words to the contrary; therefore, again I packed, and Tuesday morning the 5th of June we started on our return trip. Reached the steamer the next afternoon after several mishaps on the way due to the ignorance of our old boatman. We found quite a good sized the steamer, the *"Chong Riong,"* with a German Captain, Tessensohn by name. However, there were no accommodations for foreign passengers, but we made ourselves comfortable on deck until the soldiers arrived, and then the Captain very kindly made us take his room. We got a good room for Esther and Yousanie, and after the boat started, Sylvia staid with them, as she is so seasick she is no help with the baby then. We did not leave until Sunday the 10th, Sherwood's 7-month birthday. We were only about 27 hours in reaching Chemulpo. After getting out at sea, Doctor and I were both quite sick again, but not so sick as when we came up, and the next morning I felt as if I were on my sea legs again when I got up, but in a few hours we were in harbor. Mr. Jones met us and we went right to his house, the Koreans going to Mr. Kang's, and we were soon made very comfortable.

That afternoon, Mr. and Mrs. Jones, Doctor and I went out to see our American man of war, the *Baltimore*. It is fine; the officers were very kind and showed us all over. Rear Admiral Skerrett[144] invited us to take tea with him in his own room, and we had pleasant chats with several. I never knew so much about a man of war or the people up-

---

[144] Rear Admiral Joseph Salathiel Skerrett (1833 -1897) was an officer in the United States Navy.

on it before. The Admiral himself is a Christian and a teetotaler, and his officers all seem like such nice men. They are married with their families either at home, or else in Japan, boarding in the port where the warship is ordered to stop. When it changes its place, they cannot travel upon it, but take the next Mail Ship, if the warship is to remain in the other place any length of time. None of them came to Chemulpo, and their husbands are all so anxious to get back to Japan. But the Admiral, although he seems quite as anxious as anyone to get back to his wife and daughter, thinks that Minister Sill is not likely to let them go for some time, until matters become more settled in Korea. Why! We found 13 men of war in the harbor when we arrived, and rumors of thousands of both Japanese and Chinese soldiers landed.

It seems Korea asked China to help her quell the rebellion in the South, and China landed soldiers in Korea without letting Japan know, which was contrary to their treaty, so Japan is sending soldiers all the time now, and it looks as if the fat is in the fire and Japan and China have returned to their old battle-ground. Poor Korea, I fear she will be extinguished in the conflict.

We came to the Sŏul the next day on the same riverboat with Admiral Skerrett and Lieuts Fox and Wilson who came up to see Minister Sill. We became quite well acquainted on the way, and had a pleasant trip up.[145]

---

[145] Rosetta added later, "Also made the acquaintance of Mr. Joly and wife, British Consul. He died about the time Edith did and Mrs. Joly and I have ever had a bond of sympathy." Mr. Joly died in 1897 and was buried at Yanghwajin.

Diary of Dr. Rosetta Hall 1892-1894

At the landing whom should we meet but Dr. Busteed on his way to America to be married. Mr. Noble was going with him to Chemulpo to see him off and to visit the *Baltimore*.

We reached the house about 4 p.m. Mrs. Noble was out, but came home in about an hour.

I let Sylvia go to her brother-in-laws's after supper expecting she would return by bedtime, but she didn't come till morning, and Sherwood was sick all night, had bloody stools. They continued the next day, and we decided we were in for a siege of dysentery with him.

The next night, Wednesday night, about 12 o'clock, I was called by Mrs. Noble to her room. Mr. Noble had not yet returned. She had not been able to go to sleep on account of some constantly recurring pains, and thought she might be in labor though she did not expect to be for another week. I made an examination and found good progress had been made, the cervix being over half dilated. I fixed her bed, and sent for Miss Harris whom she had engaged as nurse, and after an easy and a very patient time of it, a little 7 pound girl was born at 6 a.m. Mrs. Noble says she is sweet and she calls her "Ruth."[146] Mr. Noble came home about p.m., very much surprised to find the new arrival. He had not heard a word of it until he stepped into the room. A pretty good joke on "Arthur and Mattie" we all think.

---

[146] Ruth Noble (1894-1986) later married Henry D. Appenzeller and served in Korea from 1917 to 1962 as a missionary. She is buried at Yanghwajin with her husband.

Diary of Dr. Rosetta Hall 1892-1894

For a whole week, Sherwood remained much the same, passing bright blood in nearly every stool. We washed out his bowels, gave him Bismuth, Pepsin, and Tr. Opii Camph[147] to no avail. He holds his own wonderfully, is so merry and laughs whenever he can get an excuse that we can't realize he is so sick. But his rosy cheeks are gone and his plump little limbs are smaller and more flabby. Dear little man, he is just as patient, and takes his medicine from a spoon so well. As he was not getting any better last Saturday, Doctor went to get Dr. Avison's advice as to a change in treatment. He advised an injection of blue Pyoktanin[148], and to give Listerine and Bichloride by the mouth. This we did over Sunday, but he was no better Monday. Dr. Avison came into see him. He advised an increased dose of the internal medicine with the addition of Ipecacuanha[149]. It makes a real strong disagreeable medicine, and Sherwood makes up a little face but takes it so good—the brave little man. Tuesday, his stool contained more pus and less blood, but still a considerable amount of bright blood would be passed altogether through the day. In the afternoon, his appetite begin to fail for the first; he only ate half his portion at 1 p.m. and would eat no more till 6 p.m., then not till 11 p.m. and no more until morning. Wednesday afternoon, he threw up in one gush the food he took at 1 p.m.,

---

[147] Tr. Opii Camph is camphorated tincture of opium, used to treat diarrhea.

[148] Blue pyoktanin is an aniline dye, also known as crystal violet or methyl violet, which was found to have "pus-killing" properties by a German ophthalmologist Jakob Stilling in 1890.

[149] The roots of ipecacuanha or "road-side sick-making plant" were used to make syrup of ipecac, a powerful emetic. De-emetinized ipecacuanha was used as an antidysenteric agent.

would take no more until 6 p.m., when he promptly threw it up again. At 11 p.m., he took food and retained it, and he has taken small quantities at intervals of from 3 to 4 hours today, and keeps it down all right. He begins to look rather pallid and feel a little weak, but he will laugh as usual if anyone smiles at him. He is so sunny-hearted, how we do love him and how we pray our Heavenly Father if it be His will to let him remain with us. I said to the Doctor last night, if Sherwood should die it seemed to me I would never want another baby, for I'd always be fearing it would also be taken away from us.

Wednesday, June 27, 1894

>If we love one another, God dwelleth in us. I Jn. iv. 12

>>No, the heart that has truly loved never forgets,
>>But as truly loves on to the close
>>As the sunflower turns on her god when he sets
>>The same look which she turned when he rose!
>>—Thomas Moore

The second anniversary of our marriage. Doctor took me on his knee this morning and between kisses tried to tell me how much he loved me. He said two years ago today he knew he was getting a treasure but he did not know how great a one, and now he begins to know in a measure; he loved me then all he thought one could, but he loves me a thousand times more today.

Diary of Dr. Rosetta Hall 1892-1894

Dear Doctor, he has just proven to be one of the very best of husbands, of course it seems to me the best, and I love him with my whole heart.

And now there is our dear little boy, how we love him, and what a sweet little man he is. He has been so sick, but he is surely better today, and we are so thankful. We are talking about getting off to Pukhan as soon as possible. It is very very hot already, and we fear Sherwood cannot get quite well here.

This afternoon, 5 p.m., Doctor and I went out for the first and called upon Rev. Lee and his new wife and mother-in-law, also upon American Minister Sill and family. He told us the good news that the word had gone from the foreign office to Pyong Yang ordering the punishment of that Governor's servant that instigated the most of the trouble, also of the acting magistrate that helped him carry it out, the punishment to take place before Mr. Moffett. They are also required to return the money extorted from Han, and are to be banished from the city. That is pretty good news, it seems as if we would have little or no trouble there hereafter. We also called at the British Legation where we were married two years ago today.

On our way home, we heard that a circular went out of the American Legation yesterday calling in Reverends Moore, Junkin, Reynolds, Tate[150], and Dr. Drew and fami-

---

[150] Rev. Lewis Boyd Tate (1862-1929) arrived in Korea in 1892 as a Southern Presbyterian missionary, married Dr. Mattie Ingold in 1905, served in Jeonju and Chongju until his retirement from the field in

Diary of Dr. Rosetta Hall 1892-1894

lies to the foreign settlement here, and that arrangements had already been made for each family among the families of the Presbyterian Missions. I feel so sorry for the married ladies for each one of the four expects a little baby this summer, and it must be so difficult for them to tear up and leave their snug homes and go to the houses of other families. It is just too bad, and I believe it will prove unnecessary, however, of course, it is best to keep on the safe side. More and more Japanese soldiers arrive, and they are strong in the city beside have stations on all the surrounding hills. There are also rumors of thousands of Chinese soldiers landing along the coast. Some say war has been declared between China and Japan. It is very difficult to forecast the outcome. However, our British Consul General Gardner says it will be all right for us to go to Pukhan when we like, and he doesn't seem to apprehend any danger for British or Americans.

I fear our people at home are pretty uneasy about us at this time, the papers filling with these rumors of war so soon after hearing of our Pyong Yang trouble. I wrote home yesterday, and must try and write often. Dear people, they will mind it much more than we do no doubt.

Well, this day has passed and gone and we will soon enter upon our third year of married life, as Doctor prayed at evening prayers, may it prove the best year we have yet seen, and may our love and happiness continue to increase as it has in the past. How good, how very good, God is to us.

1925. His sister Miss Martha Samuel Tate (1864-1940) was also a missionary to Korea for nearly 50 years.

Diary of Dr. Rosetta Hall 1892-1894

"Here closely nestled by thy side,
      Thy arm around me thrown,
I ask no more. <u>In mirth and pride,
      I 've stood — oh, so alone!</u>
Now, what is all this world to me,
      Since I have found my world in thee!

Oh, if we are so happy here,
      Amid our toils and pains,
With thronging cares and dangers near,
      And marred by earthly stains,
How great must be the compass given
      Our souls, to <u>bear </u>the bliss of heaven!"[151]

Wednesday, September 19, 1894

But the God of all grace, who hath called us unto his eternal glory by Christ Jesus, after that ye have suffered a while, make you perfect, stablish, strengthen, settle you. I Pet. v. 10

All before us lies the way;
      Give the past unto the wind:
All before us is the Day,
      Night and darkness are behind.

Eden with its angels bold,
      Love and flowers and coolest sea,
Less is ancient story told
      Than a glowing prophecy.

---

[151] An excerpt of Dr. Emily C. Judson's poem, "To My Husband," written in Rangoon, 1847

Diary of Dr. Rosetta Hall 1892-1894

> When the soul to sin hath died,
> > True and beautiful and sound,
> Then all earth is sanctified,
> > Upsprings paradise around.
> —R. W. Emerson

I am 29 years old today, so I will soon be out of the twenties into the thirties. It strange, but such is life.

After breakfast, I found a little package on my desk containing a white silk handkerchief with the best wishes of Mr. and Mrs. Pak (that is Yousanie and Esther). Doctor presented me with two beautiful Korean pillow ends with carvings in Jade. Also bought a goose to roast for my birthday dinner. Am going to have all the Pyong Yang folks here—namely, Rev. Moffett, Rev. and Mrs. Lee, Mrs. Webb[152], Doctor, little Sherwood and I.

We continue to have good news from both of our homes. God blesses them with good health. Poor old black Joe, he still worries about me. Mother writes, "Joe says tell you he don't want you to go to Pyong Yang amongst those heathen devils again, you have just escaped with your life, now keep away, God made them heathens, let them be so, if He wants them converted He has the power to do it." Quite a speech for Joe, dear old fellow, he doesn't understand God's way of converting people very well. Mother says, we all think you are having a hard time, why don't you come home? Mother speaks about prizing the letters

---

[152] Mrs. Webb is Mrs. Graham Lee (maiden name Blanche Webb)'s mother.

Diary of Dr. Rosetta Hall 1892-1894

Doctor and I write for the papers so much. Also spoke of Mrs. Smith (a sister-in-law of Thomas Lane) from the West who is much interested in Mission work, and had read a number of my articles, calling on them because she had such a desire to see my parents. Mother says, "I showed her yours and William's pictures, and the talk was mostly about you and the war in your place." It makes me smile to think of hearing Mother say "William" – guess she must have quite adopted Doctor, as her son, at last.

They are all more or less concerned about the war here in Korea. Of course they don't get very good accounts of it in the papers, and we have not dared to write much for fear it wouldn't reach them. Mr. and Mrs. Noble and Ruth went to Japan the last of August and we sent letters with them to post in Japan with more detailed news.

It has been so long since I have written in my journal that it will be difficult to write up much of the war news that has happened since, and other news too, but quite a little of it is written in Sherwood's journal in which I have written once a month.[153]

On the morning of July 23, the Japanese army took possession of the city before breakfast, don't know how many were killed or wounded, but Doctor has since had some ten or a dozen of wounded Korean soldiers to treat in the hospital. On the 20th, there was a naval engagement between the Japanese and Chinese some ways from Chemulpo. The 29th, there was a land battle in both of which the Japanese

---

[153] See the diary of August 10, 1894 in the *Journal of Sherwood Hall*.

Diary of Dr. Rosetta Hall 1892-1894

were successful, though I believe the Chinese also claim the victory. Soldiers from the gunboats of the respective countries represented here came to guard the Legations and foreign property. Everybody has been in the city all summer until recently, as it did not seem to be safe to travel by land or by water. There has been quite a little sickness. It has been a very hot summer, 100°, 102°, and even 104°, not nearly as much rain as usual. It was so hot at night in our house we couldn't sleep, so Doctor put up our tent on the school-ground so as to catch a breeze if there was any, and there we slept very well.

When we went to Pyong Yang, we broke up keeping house together with the Nobles. Since our return, we have boarded with them paying $60 (silver) a month for our board. After the Nobles went to Japan, we of course kept house on our own hook, and I think now we will continue to when they return. They, of course, wish to have a cook and boy trained of their own, so when we go to Pyong Yang they are not left without, and we want to keep Younsanie. Then now that we each have a baby, the washing and ironing will be difficult to do in one kitchen with all the other work. Beside there are even more different requirements of food now than before, and it seems as if it would be more satisfactory for both parties to have our own table. So we will make our kitchen in what were Doctor's shop, and our dining room and Doctor's study together in what was our bedroom. We have slept in our sitting room ever since last winter anyhow. That leaves Noble's four rooms, also store-room closet, and cellar. We will use the cellar some also. I shall be so glad when we can have a home of

Diary of Dr. Rosetta Hall 1892-1894

our own. I feel as if we never had yet except for the brief time when we lived at Pyong Yang, and I was so happy there, I didn't want to come back to Söul. If it hadn't been for the war, I expect we would have at least moved to Chemulpo this fall as by steamer we could work Pyong Yang much easier and cheaper with less loss of time than from Söul. As it is, however, Dr. Scranton doesn't want us to go.

We had a very pleasant time this evening, our company all came. Reverends Moffett and Lee with Doctor are planning to make a trip to Pyong Yang just as soon as satisfactory news of the impending battle arrives.

It is late and I am tired and I will not write more but close with a quotation I have been reading, and that strikes me as having the true ring in it.

> "If we could but live in constant remembrance of the great truth, that to God's infinity no actions are great or small; if we could only give up striving to do something which the *world* shall call great, and simply try to live a life with divinity in the smallest action of it, thereby making our existence one grand anthem of praise to our Creator, —in other words, if our lives could by reason of their simplicity grow more like Christ's, should we not be much happier?"
> —Lydia Huntley

Diary of Dr. Rosetta Hall 1892-1894

October 1894[154]

Monday, October 1st, Doctor left for Pyong Yang, in company with Messrs Moffett and Lee. The 8th I received telegram that they had arrived safely and the following Saturday night I received a letter written from Pyong Yang, copy of which I will place here. (For said copy see over.) In another letter Doctor said that our Christians had made a flour mill, and had supported themselves by making flour to sell to the Chinese, that on Sundays, the mill work was stopped and no flour sold. Also the day after the Japanese took the city, a Japanese Korean doctor who happened to be a Methodist hearing there were Christians at our house stopped there and conversed with Chang Sikey by means of the Chinese character, and later made it his home there in the house. Mr. Lee who went up to Pyong Yang on his bicycle got there several hours before the Doctor, and this Christian doctor and perhaps others (for there were other Japanese Christians who met with them for worship) did a very pretty thing to greet the Doctor's coming—over the gate, they placed the Japanese and American flags over a red cross and twined evergreens about all.

---

[154] Rosetta did not date this last portion of the diary, but it is likely written sometime in October, 1894.

Diary of Dr. Rosetta Hall 1892-1894

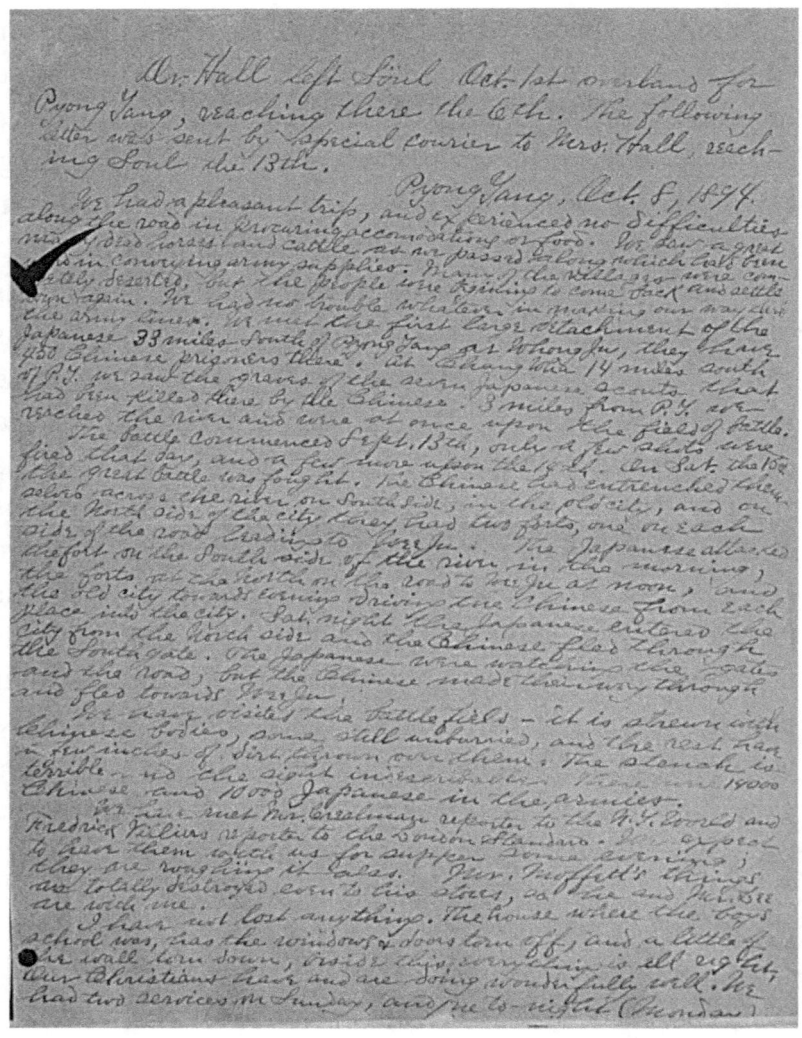

William James Hall's October 8, 1894 letter copied
and inserted by Rosetta Hall, page 1

Diary of Dr. Rosetta Hall 1892-1894

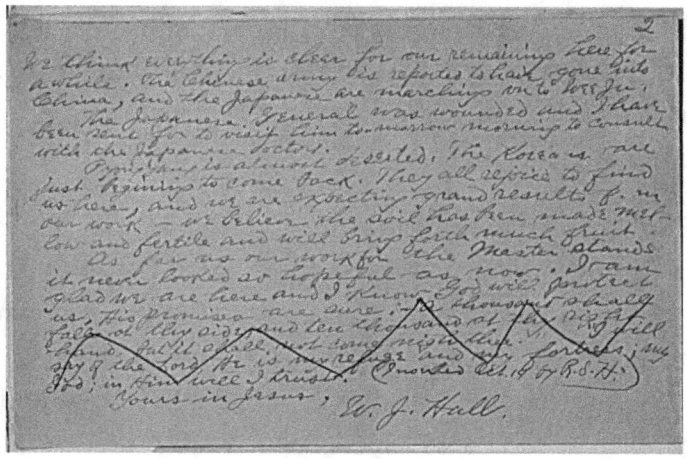

William James Hall's October 8, 1894 letter, page 2

Dr. Hall left Söul Oct. 1st overland for Pyong Yang, reaching there the 6th. The following letter was sent by special courier to Mrs. Hall, reaching Söul the 13th.

Pyong Yang,
Oct. 8, 1894

We had a pleasant trip, and experienced no difficulties along the road in procuring accommodations or food. We saw a great many dead horses and cattle as we passed along which had been used in conveying army supplies. Many of the villages were completely deserted, but the people were beginning to come back and settle down again. We had no trouble whatsoever in making our way through the army lines. We met the first large detachment of the Japanese 33 miles south of Pyong Yang at Whang Ju, they have 450 Chinese prisoners there. At Chung Wha 14 miles

Diary of Dr. Rosetta Hall 1892-1894

south of P.Y. we saw the graves of the seven Japanese scouts that had been killed there by the Chinese. 3 miles from P.Y. we reached the river and were at once upon the field of battle.

The battle commenced Sept. 13th, only a few shots were fired that day, and a few more upon the 14th. On Sat. the 15th, the great battle was fought. The Chinese had entrenched themselves across the river on South side, in the old city, and on the North side of the city they had two forts, one on each side of the road leading to Wee Ju. The Japanese attacked the fort on the South side of the river in the morning, the forts at the North on the road to Wee Ju at noon, and the old city towards evening driving the Chinese from each place into the city. Sat. night, the Japanese entered the city from the North side and the Chinese fled through the South gate. The Japanese were watching the gates and the road, but the Chinese made their way through and fled towards Wee Ju.

We have visited the battlefield, it is strewn with Chinese bodies, some still unburied, and the rest have a few inches of dirt thrown all over them. The stench is terrible and the sight indescribable. There were 14,000 Chinese and 10,000 Japanese in the armies.

We have met Mr. Crealinau reporter to the *New York World*[155] and Fredrick Villiers reporter to the *London Standard*. We expect to have them with us for supper some evening; they are roughing it also. Mr. Moffett's things are

---

[155] The *New York World* was a **newspaper** published in New York City from 1860 until 1931.

Diary of Dr. Rosetta Hall 1892-1894

totally destroyed even to his stores, so he and Mr. Lee are with me.

I have not lost anything. The house where the boys school was, I has the windows and doors torn off, and a little of the wall torn down, beside this, everything is all right. Our Christians have and are doing wonderfully well. We had two services on Sunday, and one tonight (Monday). We think everything is clear for our remaining here for a while. The Chinese army is reported to have gone into China, and the Japanese are marching on to Wee Ju.

The Japanese General was wounded and I have been sent for to visit him tomorrow morning to consult with the Japanese doctors.

Pyong Yang is almost deserted. The Koreans are just beginning to come back. They all rejoice to find us here, and we are expecting grand results for our work. We believe the soil has been made mellow and fertile and will bring forth much fruit.

As far as our work for the Master stands, it never looked so hopeful as now. I am glad we are here and I know God will protect us. Hiss promises are sure. "A thousand shall fall at thy side and ten thousand at thy right hand, but it shall not come nigh thee."[156] "I will say of the Lord, He is my refugee and my fortress; my God; in Him will I trust."[157]

---

[156] Psalm 91:7.
[157] Psalm 91:2.

Diary of Dr. Rosetta Hall 1892-1894

Yours in Jesus,

W. J. Hall

(Inserted October 14 by R. S. H.)

MEMORIAL SERVICE[158]

Rev. William James Hall M.D.

Pai Chai Chapel

November 27, 1894

Hymn. — No. 979 Methodist Hymnal. — "Asleep in Jesus."

Scripture Lesson. — Isaiah 43:1-15 :Rev. W. B. Scranton, M.D.

Prayer.:

Hymn of Fanny Crosby

Address. — Biographical. Rev. W.A. Noble

Address. — Dr. Vinton. Dr. Hall as a Medical Missionary.

Address. — Rev. S. A. Moffett

Hymn. — No. 234 Gospel Hymns. — "Consecration."[159]

---

[158] Dr. William James Hall contracted typhus fever on his way back home, died on November 24, 1894, one week after his arrival to Seoul. The following is Dr. Rosetta Hall's transcription of her husband's letter sent to her. For more details, see Dr. Rosetta Hall's *Journal of Sherwood Hal* and *Journal of Edith Margaret Hall*.

Diary of Dr. Rosetta Hall 1892-1894

Address. — Dr. Busteed.

Address. — Rev. Graham Lee.

Hymn. — No. 314 Gospel Hymns. — "My Jesus I love Thee."

Address. — Dr. Hall's Introduction to Mission Work and End. Rev. H. G. Appenzeller.

Solo. — "Sweeping through the Gates."[160] Rev. Graham Lee. (Congregation will join in chorus.)

                Benediction.

A Letter to 121 Girls[161] Written by Rosetta on her 5th Wedding Anniversary

Liberty, New York
Monday, June 28, 1897

Dear girls of 121,

    We forgot to look at the calendar to see what day "June 27th" came on, and as five years ago this time it fell upon Monday, I thought I would choose today rather than Saturday as some of you may do instead of Sunday.

    It is a most beautiful June day —

---

[159] "Take My Life and Let It Be" by Frances Ridley Havergal.
[160] Also known as "Washed in the Blood of the Lamb," words and music by Rev. Tullius C. O'Kane (1830-1912).
[161] Likely Rosetta's medical school circle.

Diary of Dr. Rosetta Hall 1892-1894

"And what is so rare as a day in June?
    Then, if ever, come perfect days;
Then Heaven tries the earth if it be in tune
    And over it softly her warm ear lays;
Whether we look, or whether we listen
    We hear life murmur, or see it glisten."

  I suppose the sky is just as blue, the grass is just as green, and the flowers as bright and gay, as they were five years ago upon my wedding day, but somehow it is less easy to realize.

When some beloved voice that was to you
Both sound and sweetness, faileth suddenly,
And silence against which you dare not cry,
Arches round you like a strong disease and new
— What hope? What help? What music will undo
That silence to your sense?
—E. B. Browning

Appendix 1

Mission Report by Rosetta Sherwood Hall to Dr. Leonard, December 14, 1892[162]

Seoul, Korea
December 14, 1892

Dear Dr. Leonard,

Since our Annual Meeting the last of August when the Bishop reappointed me to the medical work in the Woman's Hospital, I have treated 1329 dispensary patients, admitted 18 into the wards, and have made 42 professional outcalls. A number of books and Sunday sheets have been sold and some given away. Dispensary receipts $20.

The average attendance of the Sunday afternoon service in the Dispensary has been 23. Miss Lewis now plays the organ at this meeting, and it proves a help that we have not had in these services before.

The building upon the ground purchased of the Parent Board has been remodeled and we have from it three small wards that are neat and nice, and a valuable addition to our property.

The new dispensary in connection with the Baldwin Chapel at the East Gate will soon be finished, and soon after Christmas I hope to open medical work there. It is just across the city upon the other side from the hospital and promises to a good field for the much-needed work.

---

[162] Missionary Files: Methodist Episcopal Church; Missionary Correspondence, 1846-1912, Microfilm S3458, Reel 16, No. 0529.

Diary of Dr. Rosetta Hall 1892-1894

We have some new Korean Helpers in the Hospital who are proving very valuable. For some time I have been trying to secure the services of a suitable young widow to train to help in the work as upon account of the early marriage custom we must expect to soon lose the school-girls we have trained. After Annual Meeting, I learned of a young widow in the No Family of our church and found her quite willing to come and make a trial of the work: she enjoys it very much and is proving a real help. "Susan," as she has been baptized, is in the school all the morning, and is making the very best use of her time; she could read but very little when she came to us but now reads her Bible readily, and can write a nice letter in Korean: it is interesting to watch how bright her face is growing, and how her Christian character is developing.

Then, too, we have now "Mary," one of our married school-girls for Matron and Bible woman in the hospital. Mary felt called of God to this work, and is very happy in it. Her sweet face and winning ways bring her into favor at once with the people; and I am convinced she will prove a great power for good to them.

One of the little girls from the school has been our most serious case for some time in the hospital; she was taken with capillary bronchitis which rapidly ran into catarrhal pneumonia but God has blessed the means used to her recovery, and she will soon be able to return to school. Among the present inpatients are two little motherless waifs, one aged four years, the other but six-month-old, who were both brought to us in a starving condition, and needed good food and nursing rather medicine. Both are thriving well now, and it is a pleasure to watch them improve.

Diary of Dr. Rosetta Hall 1892-1894

During the last three months many of my outcalls have been to the houses of those of rank--among others at two different "*Pansyo*"s (판서). At one of these places (this is the home of the grandchildren of the former King's daughter) afterward they invited me to visit them socially on a certain day and to bring with me Mary who is a fair interpreter. Miss Lewis also went, and we took our Korean hymn books and Bible. Miss Lewis and Mary sang several hymns, and Mary read and explained a selection from Acts XVI. The lady of the house (부인, *Puene*), her little daughter, and two "Palace women" who were present beside a lot of women servants and children all listened with intense interest. Later when they brought us each a table loaded with Korean food and confection, I told them it was the Christian custom to thank God for our food before eating, so we all bowed in prayer for a few moments led by Mary. I have been to this house twice since to visit a child with a broken femur in the servants quarters, and each time was urged to go in to visit the Puene, but had time but once.

I was called out one Sunday morning to the house of a former patient whose little boy lay in convulsions. After examining him carefully and giving the needed medicine, I asked the Grandmother who has often been to our Sunday services, to pray for the little patient which she did in the following simple manner: "O, God, save the five-year-old child. O, God, save the five-year-old child"—repeating this earnestly many times with tears in her eyes. The Lord did spare the child, and the whole family were very grateful. Since then for over a month now, Miss Lewis and I have gone to this house regularly once a week to read, sing and pray with them, and they receive us always with delight. It is a "well-to-do" family, The grandmother, mother, and daughter all read. Miss Lewis trying to teach the children to sing – they both know the words of "There is a Happy

Land," now. The last time I was there the little girl, Pope ("보비") by name, told me her "grandmother prayed every day and never once forgot." I am in hopes this household may soon desire to receive baptism.

We are always received so gladly into any of the homes where we have been called professionally that I am sure as soon as we are able to follow up this work there will be far greater results. I trust we may soon have more workers in the field, so that there maybe better opportunity to study the language and more time to do evangelistic work in the homes whose doors are being opened so wide to receive us.

Yours in the Master's work,

Rosetta Sherwood Hall, M.D.

Appendix 2

Mission Report by William James Hall to Dr. Leonard, December 21, 1892[163]

Soul, Korea
December 21, 1892

Dear Dr. Leonard,

On the 21st of September after loading my ponies with books and drugs I started on my journey to the north. I stopped at Song Do for two days, a city of about 50,000 inhabitants and situated to 160 li north of Seoul. I treated a number of patients and sold 62 Christian books. I have also started work at Whang Chu, a city containing about 16,000 inhabitants and 450 li from Seoul. I also want open up work at Pong San Pop about 4500 [inhabitants] and 110 li from Seoul, and at Saw Hung Pop, 3000 [inhabitants] and 340 li from Seoul and [at] On Chu 650 li from Seoul.

But at present I am giving the most of my time to Pyong Yang, a city 550 li from Seoul and containing a population of about 45,000. This could form a centre from which On Chu, Whang Chu, Pong San and Saw Hung could be worked. Song Do can be reached from Seoul. The natives have shown me great kindness and the prospects for work in the interior are very encouraging.

---

[163] Missionary Files: Methodist Episcopal Church; Missionary Correspondence, 1846-1912, Microfilm S3458, Reel 16, No. 0529.

Diary of Dr. Rosetta Hall 1892-1894

Last spring when I made my first trip to the north in company with Brother Jones, the governor issued an edict prohibiting the people buying superstitious books, after which they stopped buying our books. But on my two trips this fall, I have not met with the slightest opposition and the people appeared anxious to buy and read our books, of which I have sold 603 copies.

Our medical work brings us into great favor with the people. I have treated 588 patients. I have had a little room, 8 ft.^{2}, in which to take my meals, sleep, treat my patients, sell books and hold our meetings. We are in great need of a suitable building for dispensary, hospital, chapel, book store, and dwelling, and we are claiming the promise. Philippians 4:19. But my God shall supply all of your need. The work is His and His interest in it is far greater than ours can possibly be. He can and will open up our way before us.

On my first trip, I have called to see a little boy the son of an employee of the governor, who had fallen and injured his hip. The Korean doctor had inserted a needle and an abscess had formed; there was also an abscess on the lower part of each leg. His legs were also swollen from drapery and he was in a very emaciated state. I treated him each day I was in Pyong Yang and when I came away he was much improved. The parents appeared very grateful and made me several presents. I was very sorry to leave him as I was afraid that when treatment was stopped, he would be back where I had found him. I left them some medicine and came away. After nearly four weeks, I returned and upon visiting my little friend, I found he had quite recov-

Diary of Dr. Rosetta Hall 1892-1894

ered. The gratitude of the parents knew no bounds. They gave up the two comfortable rooms they were living in for me to occupy during my stay in Pyong Yang and told me to use anything they had the same as if I were in my own home. They did everything in their power to entertain me. I asked my friend if he knew of any house that I could purchase that would be suitable for our work. After a few days he said he had looked over the city and could not find any house that would be as suitable as his and offered to let me have it. I was quite surprised as it was such a valuable piece of property and situated in one of the most desirable localities of the city.

It is a large tile house situated on the top of a hill near the centre of the city and still far enough away from the great mass of the houses to give us good air. The plat[form] of ground is 104 feet long and 102 feet wide. The house contains about 35 kan (a kan is about 8 ft.^{2}) and is just what we need for our work. There is room for two dispensaries, one for women and the other for men, a chapel, book store, and dwelling. But we have not a single cent appropriated for the the purchase of property in Pyong Yang. When our estimates were made out, we did not know that there would be any opening in Pyong Yang and we all feel the necessity of taking advantage of this open door, and that the opening is of the Lord and we are going forward until He blocks our way. The house is offered to us for 780 yen and we need 4 small houses in the back which would give us an opening to the street and give us nearly the whole brow of the hill. These will cost about 200 yen, or the both pieces of property would cost seven hundred dollars gold

Diary of Dr. Rosetta Hall 1892-1894

($700). If the Board will grant $350 gold, I will become responsible for the balance. May I have the privilege of raising some money among my friends in America and applying it to any work here, if I make a report of all to the Board? Could it be sent directly to me or must it come through the Board?

A good number in Pyong Yang are deeply interested in Christianity and we are looking to God for glorious results. In Him we are never disappointed. Where He leads we will follow and for whatever He gives we will ascribe to Him all the glory.

I have been assured by those who know most about Korea and Koreans that we are running very little risk in purchasing property in the interior, if we have the deed drawn up in the name of a Korean and then hold the deed in our position. And the people are so friendly towards us and more especially so with our medical work that I don't think there will be the slightest opposition.

Dr. Scranton has about 15 probationers that he soon expects to baptize, and ernest inquirers are coming to him every day. Brother Ohlinger's work is encouraging. I assisted him in baptizing six natives December 11. Mrs. Jones is doing a good work at Chemulpo. Dr. McGill has been on a trip to Wonsan, from which he gives encouraging report. Brother Noble is doing good work in the school and at the language. My offer to become responsible for one half of Dr. Busteed's salary for two years will hold good if he is sent within a year. How I wish he were here now so he could get a start on the language before he would be overwhelmed with the work.

Yours in Jesus,

W. J. Hall

Appendix 3

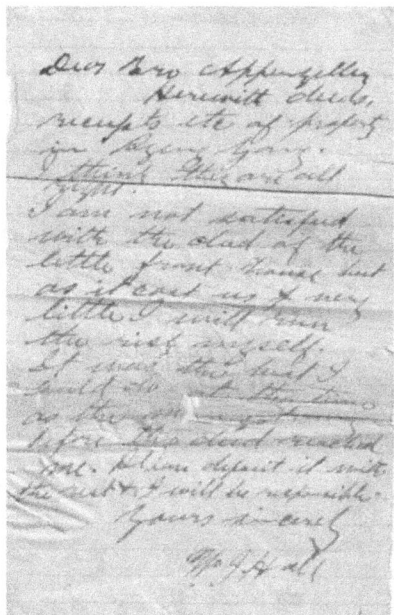

Letter Written by Rev. William J. Hall, M.D. to Rev. Henry G. Appenzeller, c. March 1893[164]

Dear Brother Appenzeller,

Herewith deeds, receipts etc. of property in Pyeng Yang. I think they are all right. I am not satisfied with the deed of the little front house but as it cost us very little I will run the risk myself. It was the best I could do at the time as the

---

[164] Keepsakes from the Hall Family. Donated to the Yanghwajin Institute.

Diary of Dr. Rosetta Hall 1892-1894

man got away before the deed reached me. Please deposit it with the rest and I will be responsible.

Yours sincerely,

W. J. Hall

Appendix 4

Mission Report by William James Hall to Dr. Leonard, April 12, 1893[165]

Seoul, Korea
April 12, 1893

A. B. Leonard, D.D.
Corresponding Secretary, Mission Rooms
New York City, USA

Dear Dr. Leonard,

Your letter of January 26, also of February 23 written to Dr. Hall both received--the latter with note of Exchange for $40, and the good news that Dr. Busteed will soon be sent, also that Doctor may purchase the property upon the terms stated. Doctor is not yet back from Pyong Yang and We Chu—he has been gone nearly two months, and I think will soon return when he will write you in person.

I trust you received the Doctor's letter, written just before he went away this last time, in regard to settling with Mrs. Skidmore for my passage and outfit money, and that before now it has all been arranged for.

Dr. Mary Cutler has arrived, and we like her very much. I am still continuing to attend to all the work except when I

---

[165] Missionary Files: Methodist Episcopal Church; Missionary Correspondence, 1846-1912, Microfilm S3458, Reel 16, No. 0529.

Diary of Dr. Rosetta Hall 1892-1894

go over to the Baldwin Dispensary at the East Gate, Dr. Cutler takes the dispensary here. I am anxious to give her a better opportunity for study of the language, now from the start, than I have ever had.

I notice in the Heathen Woman's Friend for March that it says Dr. Cutler "goes to Korea, to take up the medical work left unprovided for by the marriage of Dr. Sherwood." I think that a very misleading statement and trust the dear ladies of the W.F.M.S. will find it so someday. My work has been continued ever since my marriage just as before. Last month I treated over 600 cases, the most I have treated in any one month since I have been here. Instead of leaving the work unprovided for, I have not only cared for the work already started but opened new work upon the other side of the city at the Baldwin Dispensary. Well, never mind, it is hard pleasing some people, but then that is not what I am working for. The work progresses all the same, though it is a bit discouraging to the worker.

I will enclose a little article written by Mrs. Noble, that I think you might like to send to the "World Wide Missions" or "Gospel in All Lands" for publication, though it was not written with that object in view. You know perhaps Rev. and Mrs. Noble live with Dr. Hall and myself in Mr. Appenzeller's house. Expect we will have to get out soon, as the Appenzeller's will be returning.

Dr. Hall and myself are in hopes that we may both be sent to Pyong Yang this fall, that I may start medical work for women, while he goes on with his work. We find it a pretty hard trial to be separated so much, but we are trying to bear it bravely for the work's sake.

Very truly yours,

Mrs. W. J. Hall

We have missed "World Wide Missions" since the December number. You spoke about sending Doctor's letter to it for publication, would like to see it.

Diary of Dr. Rosetta Hall 1892-1894

Appendix 5

Pioneer Medical Missionary Work in the Interior Korea[166]

My dear Dr. Leonard,

On the 20th of February accompanied by Mr. Noble, I started upon my fourth missionary tour in the northern interior of Korea. Our little pack ponies were well loaded with books and medicines and a little foreign food. The weather was still cold and although we were quite well equipped we suffered considerably. The rivers were frozen so we could cross them on ice.

One cold morning we came to a man lying in the road. At first we thought he was sick or drunk, but upon the closer examination, we found he was dead and frozen stiff. The natives passed by without paying any attention to what seemed to us such a terrible sight. We tried to find out all we could about the case and learned that the poor man have been sick, was without home or friends, and being unable to go farther, and as the night was bitter cold he had frozen to death. When the sick are without friends here they have a hard time, often they are put out on the city wall to die, and frequently we find them before it is too late and take them to the hospital where they are clothed

---

[166] Undated, but likely written in May 1893 after 2 months of travelling to northern Korea from February to April. Missionary Files: Methodist Episcopal Church; Missionary Correspondence, 1846-1912, Microfilm S3458, Reel 16, No. 0529.

Diary of Dr. Rosetta Hall 1892-1894

and fed, and with proper treatment in a good room they soon recover. Many precious lives are saved in this way and led to Christ.

We traveled about 30 miles each day, and as our pack ponies could not go fast we walked most of the time in order to keep warm. Upon arriving at the inns often we would find them very cold and at other times too hot. The vermin troubled us a great deal although not so much as in warm weather. The diet was very unpalatable but hunger soon enabled us to consume a good portion.

After six days travel we reached Pyong Yang 180 miles from Soul. We at once went to a friend's house where I had been entertained last fall. He was one of the governor's assistants and last summer I was called to treat his son who was in a dying condition. God blessed the means and speedily restored the boy to health. The gratitude of the parents knew no bounds. They made me several presents of eggs, chickens and ducks. When I returned in the fall I was invited into their home, and given a very pleasant room. What an agreeable change! from the filthy inn where I had been stopping in a room 8 ft. square, in which I had treated my patients one by one.

Our new friend manifested a deep interest in Christianity and would frequently come in late at night after his duties at the governor's office were done and we would talk of the things of God until midnight and then we would kneel together and pour out our hearts to God. We are looking for good results from this seed sowing. When I went back

Diary of Dr. Rosetta Hall 1892-1894

the second time he said he was more glad to see me than he would be to see his parents, and he wanted me to use everything he had just the same as if it were my own.

Through our native helper we were able to get a place well situated for our work, which I trust will soon be our hospital. As it was in a different section of the city from where I had been before the people did not know me and they felt uneasy over my presence, and went to the governor and asked him to remove the foreigner as they were much afraid. The governor replied, "The foreigner is not a bad man but a gentleman. He cares the sick and helps the poor, is he not a good man?" He gave orders to the captain in charge of the district I was in to quiet the people and arrest any giving me trouble. Their fears were allayed and soon my hands were filled with patients flocking from all part of the city and surrounding country. Long before the appointed time, they would gather on the street in front of the dispensary and wait until the hour arrived.

Before I left Pyong Yang I was treating over 60 patients daily. Others would come for me with chairs carried by coolies and take me to their homes to see the sick unable to come to the dispensary. The nearly every patient bought a Christian book and appeared to be deeply interested in Christianity. We held services with the patients before treating them; and each night and upon Sunday we gathered those together who appeared interested and further instructed them.

Since returning to Soul I have received letters urging me to

Diary of Dr. Rosetta Hall 1892-1894

return as soon as I could, that those I had taught met together every Sunday and read the Bible and prayed to God. Others have come the whole distance, six days journey on foot, for medicine for their friends.

How much we need more workers so that we could stay long with the people instructing them in the Truth. But we did all we could and will leave the results to Him to whom all power belongeth in Heaven and in earth.

After reaching Pyong Yang we had made only one fourth of our tour. We went 170 miles farther north, treating the sick, preaching the Gospel and selling Christian books in the cities and towns, through which we passed. Many expressed a desire to be Christians.

In We Chu, we had stopped nearly a week before we knew the danger to which we were exposed by our room having just previously been occupied by small-pox patients. In our journeyings, the pack ponies often fell and threw us to the ground. In one place, going over a steep mountain-pass, I was walking behind the pony when it commenced to slide, and soon fell over backwards rolling with the pack on its back to the base of the mountain! There was just room for me to step aside in a cleft to let it pass by or I would have been crushed. Strange to say the pony appeared but little injured and was able to travel on with us with its load.

The hardships, dangerous, and privations of the missionary appears as nothing compared with the joy of carrying the blessed tidings of salvation to the lost. We feel that God

Diary of Dr. Rosetta Hall 1892-1894

has a special care over missionaries and suffers no harm to befall them. Oh, that those who are His may place themselves where God can make the most use of their lives in His service.

"Not for ease or worldly pleasure

Nor for fame, my prayer shall be,
Gladly will I toil and suffer,
Only let me walk with Thee."[167]

Yours sincerely,

W. J. Hall

---

[167] From "Thou, My Everlasting Portion" by Fanny Crosby.

Diary of Dr. Rosetta Hall 1892-1894

Appendix 6

Woman's Medical Missionary Work[168]

By Rosetta Sherwood Hall, M.D., Seoul, Korea

The healing hand preparing the way for the saving Word continues to be an encouraging part of our work in Korea. At our annual meeting in 1892 Bishop Mallalieu re-appointed me in charge of the woman's hospital here in the capital of Korea. It is the first hospital for women in this country, and in it during the past year it has been my privilege to treat 6260 cases ; 119 of these were cared for in the hospital wards, 2125 were dispensary patients' first visits, 3495 were their return visits and 531 were calls to patients in their homes. The aggregate number of cases treated during my three years here is over 14,000. The records show a gain the second year over the first in round numbers of 1500, and of the third year over the second of more than 2000. Women and children from all classes of Koreans are included in these numbers, though, of course, as it is not the custom for women of the higher classes to appear upon the streets, the majority are from the low-class people. However, often quite high ladies come in closed chairs to the hospital and a good proportion of the outcalls are made upon the higher class, including several of the highest official families in the land. All patients hear .more or less of the Gospel, and many buy books and study for themselves.

---

[168] *Chinese Recorder*, Vol. 25, April 1894,167-170.

Diary of Dr. Rosetta Hall 1892-1894

Our daily services before dispensing have been more interesting than usual this year, as Miss Lewis has had more time to devote to them, and Mary Whoang, our new Korean matron, having had a good training in our girl's school, makes an instructive Bible-woman. Next year Mary will keep record of the attendance upon these meetings, as it no doubt varies from that of the dispensary, for often accompanying one patient will be two or three friends, or if the patient be from the official class there may be a half-dozen servants with her. Miss Lewis has had the entire Ross Catechism written in large plain character all around the waiting room, and this proves instructive to those who read. Sometimes one reads to the others who cannot. Upon an average hardly one in five of my women patients can read their own native language.

1 opened two new dispensaries this year - one at the East Gate and one near the South Gate of the city. The former is known as the Baldwin Dispensary, so named in honor of her who first gave toward woman's work in Korea. This place will in time prove a great blessing to the East side of the city, but it needs to have a doctor and a teacher living there. It is three miles across the city from the hospital. I go there in a Korean chair, or palanquin, which has a wooden framework of about 3x3x3 ft., and is covered with cloth upon the top and sides. A wooden grating forms the floor, upon which I sit. The front can be raised or fastened down as one pleases, and has a little window as has also each side. Extending before and behind from the bottom of the chair are two poles, by means of which two men carry it. They may only take hold of the

Diary of Dr. Rosetta Hall 1892-1894

poles with their hands, but as a rule they wear a sort of rope harness that drops from the shoulders and loops over the poles. It takes an hour to thus travel the three miles, as the chair coolies always set me down while they rest, at least twice upon the way. Sometimes I close my eyes upon the squalid mud huts and the naked children, and imagine I am being borne swiftly along upon an elevated car to my work in a home city, but the odors, ever arising from the filthy streets, soon rudely awaken me from such daydreams.

I think I have told you before of the sad results that often follow treatment by the native doctor in Korea. This year, for the first time, I saw one of them at his work, and I will try to tell you about it. I was called one day to the house of one of the higher class to see a child who had become very sick two or three days before, after being carried a long distance, strapped to the back of his nurse as is their custom, his bare head and the nape of his neck exposed to the fierce heat of a July sun. I found him in convulsions, and after a careful examination I told the father I feared there was little or no hope of his recovery. Both father and mother bowed before me and begged me to "give life," as they express it here. I told them only God could do that, but we would do all that we could, and I left them medicine and the necessary directions with the promise to return in the morning. Now this child was the only son of these people, and their love for him was just as strong as that of fond American or English parents, and like them they wanted to leave nothing undone that could be done for their darling. They had sent for the Korean doctor be-

Diary of Dr. Rosetta Hall 1892-1894

fore they called me, and when they saw the child surely growing worse they thought they would try the foreign doctor, but now as morning dawned and no improvement was visible they again sent for the Korean doctor, who arrived shortly after I did. The mother and Esther, who accompanied me, had then to leave the room, as no Korean woman may be seen by a man who does not belong to her own family. After examining the little boy I told the father that he was dying. I could do no more for him, that God was surely going to take him very soon to His Heavenly home. Then the father bade the Korean doctor to again try his skill. The first thing this doctor did was to make a little pyramid of a brownish-looking powder upon each breast of the child, and then to set it on fire; as it began to burn the tender skin I begged the father to have it removed, and I said to the doctor, " You know it can do no good," but he only calmly smiled, as he obeyed the now almost frantic father to go on with his treatment. He then took out from its sheath a needle half way between a darning-needle and a surgeon's probe in appearance, and this he proceeded to stick through each little foot, through the palms of the hands, the thumb joints and through the lip into the jaw just beneath the nose. Again I tried to make him stop, but he said it was "Korean custom." I replied, " It is a very bad custom, that though in this case it would result in no further harm, as the child was dying, yet it was exceedingly cruel, and in cases where recovery from the disease might occur inflammations of these punctured joints were sure to follow, and often suppuration with death of the bones, so that amputation of the foot or hand is the only radical cure - that many such cases had come to me at the hospital." The doctor and father now went out, and the mother and Esther came in. Esther had been telling her about our Father in heaven, and that her dear little son would soon be with Him and be free from sickness and pain for evermore. The poor mother seemed anxious to learn all she could. We prayed with her and left the little tract called "Communion" for her to read, or, as it is in Korean, "Comforting Words." A few days later she sent a servant with the message that the child had died and was buried; she sent me a little present with an invitation to visit her again, and I am sorry that as yet I have not had time to do so. There are many such doors open to receive us, but our workers are so few that we have not been able to enter them except in a few cases. When we have been able to do so the mothers, grandmothers and children have often learned to read the Bible, to sing and to pray, and those who could come out from their homes and attend the services have desired and received baptism.

We have recently finished the ninth annual meeting of the Korean M.E. Mission, Bishop Foster presiding. Dr. Leonard and Mrs. Keen, missionary secretaries, were also with us, and our work is laid out for another year. Dr. Hall and I have both been appointed to Pyong-yang, a city of the Northern interior, 180 miles from Seoul. Last year doctor was the first to be appointed to exclusive work in the interior, and now I have the privilege of being the first woman appointed to similar work. As you can imagine it is a little hard for me to give up the growing work in Seoul and my Korean girl helpers, who have grown so dear to me in these three years of training, but it is a satisfaction to be

Diary of Dr. Rosetta Hall 1892-1894

able to leave all to the good care of Dr. Mary Cutler, who came to us last April, and of Miss Lewis, who has been here nearly two years now. I am happy to go, and with our Father's help to try to build up a similar work in the still darker city of Pyong-yang, known as the "Sodom of Korea."

> "Over and over, yes deeper and deeper,
> My heart is pierced through with life's sorrowing cry;
> But the tears of the sower and the songs of the reaper
> Shall mingle together in joy by and by."[169]

---

[169] From "The Songs of the Reaper" by William A. Spencer.

Appendix 7

Pioneer Medical Missionary Work in the Interior Korea[170]

By Rev. W. J. Hall, M.D.
[M. E. Mission, Seoul, Korea.]

On the 4th of May Mrs. Hall, baby and I left Chemulpo by steamer for Pyong-yang. We had only been out a few hours when we encountered a typhoon, and were obliged to anchor for thirty-three hours. Monday afternoon we reached Po-san, which is twenty-five miles from Pyong-yang and as near the city as the steamer goes. We took a native row boat for the rest of our journey, and arrived Tuesday noon. The native Christians were waiting on the shore to greet us. Shortly after our arrival great numbers of natives came to see us. Mrs. Hall told them she would see them Wednesday afternoon. By noon hundreds of women and children had gathered in the road and outside yard to see Mrs. Hall and baby. We arranged to let them in by tens to remain for five minutes. This worked well for a short time, but soon those behind became impatient, commenced to crowd, broke down the gate, and soon the inside yard and the house were filled to overflowing. The only thing now to do was for Mrs. Hall to come outside with our little boy, where she saw yard after yard full until over fifteen hundred women and children had been seen. As we could no longer control the people I went to the magistrate and asked for a soldier

---

[170] *Chinese Recorder*, Vol. 25, September 1894, 431-433.

Diary of Dr. Rosetta Hall 1892-1894

to protect us. He promised to send one the next day, but none ever came.

About one o'clock Thursday morning we were awakened by two of the native Christians, who informed us that our faithful helper Chang Si-key and the former owner of the house we were stopping in had been cast into prison. We could do nothing then but commit them to God. Early in the morning I went to the governor's, but he was sleeping, and I could not see him. I then went to the prison and found that in addition to our men the helper of Mr. Moffett, of the Presbyterian Mission, also the former owner of the house that the helper lived in were both in prison, and that same night policemen had gone to where Mr. Moffett stopped when in Pyong- yang and cruelly beat all the native Christians that were there. Chang Si-key had his feet wedged in stocks, and was suffering intense pain. I then went to the house to see if Mrs. Hall was all right, when Mr. 0., one of our Christians who had accompanied me to the governor's, was seized and taken off to prison. Mr. Yi, another of our native Christians, then accompanied me on my rounds to the prison house and telegraph office. He would say to me : "I will be taken to prison next, and then you'll have to go alone." We were the only foreigners in a city of one hundred thousand heathen, and you can imagine our situation when I had to leave Mrs. Hall and little Sherwood alone and unprotected as much of the time I was away at the prison or the telegraph office.

I telegraphed the state of affairs to Dr. Scrauton in Seoul, and he and Mr. Moffett carried the matter to the British and American Legations, and soon the welcome message

Diary of Dr. Rosetta Hall 1892-1894

came over the wires: "Legations will act at once." No time was lost in Seoul. The missionaries and the Legations acted with that characteristic zeal, for which Britishers and Americans are noted. Soon there came a telegram from Mr. Gardner, British Consul-General, and Mr. Sill, American Minister resident stating they had insisted that the foreign office order the release of the men in prison at once, and our protection according to treaty. A telegram also came from Mr. Moffett: "Joshua first chapter ninth verse." This was Thursday evening; that night our house was stoned and the wall torn down. We did not know the moment a mob might be upon us. Early Friday morning a servant of the governor's came, and said the telegram from the king had been received, but that it said we were bad people and to kill all the Christians. I went to the prison, and this report was confirmed there. Our men had been removed to the death-cell, the torturing continued: they expected to die, but would not give up Christ.

The water carriers were forbidden to bring us water. There are no wells in Pyong-yang, and the water is brought from the river a half-mile distant. The governor is a relative of the queen, a powerful family here in Korea, and it began to look as if he were not going to pay any attention to the telegram from the foreign office. It seemed to us that the time had come for religious toleration for Korea, and God would require the lives of some of His children to secure it. We were ready to die for His cause. Grace had been given sufficient for every trial thus far, and we knew abundance would be given if it were required. My heart ached as I witnessed our faithful brothers in Christ suffering ex-

Diary of Dr. Rosetta Hall 1892-1894

treme torture, such as had not been experienced here by Christians for twenty- eight years when thousands of Roman Catholics, including several priests, laid down their lives for their faith. Two telegrams from the foreign office had been sent since Thursday night, but five o'clock Friday came, and still no relief At six o'clock, after thirty- six hours of torture in prison, threatened many times with death, all were sent for by the magistrate, beaten and discharged, but stoned all the way home. Chang Si -key was so badly injured it was with difficulty he reached home. I felt like sitting at his feet; such a faithful martyr for Jesus I had never before seen.

Messrs. Moffett and McKenzie started Friday from Seoul as a relief party; travelling day and night they reached us the following Tuesday. A week later, Dr. Scranton arrived. He and Mr. McKenzie returned the next week.

We remained in Pyong-yang a month after the difficulty arose, treating patients daily, both myself and Mrs. Hall ; we had from twenty to thirty a day. We held services Sundays and every night. Our last Sunday there 1 had twenty men, and Mrs. Hall had seven women at the service. The interest in Christianity is deepening. God is removing the obstacles and clearing away the rubbish for a harvest of souls in Pyong-yang.

The people as a rule are friendly toward us. The instigators of the trouble were some of the officials and their servants. There has just been secured through the foreign office an order demanding the restoration of the money extorted from those who were in prison and the punishment of the guilty parties. On the vessel upon which we returned there were 400 Pyong-yang soldiers, and when we reached Chemulpo we found thirteen gun-boats in the harbor, mostly Japanese and Chinese. Trouble is threatening between China and Japan, and there is strong probability of their using Korea as their battle-ground. What the outcome will be we do not know. We are looking forward to that glad day when the nations of the earth shall learn war no more.

Timeline of Dr. Rosetta Sherwood Hall (1865 – 1951)

1865	9.19	Born in Liberty, New York
		Mother: Phoebe Gildersleeve Sherwood Father: Rosevelt Rensler Sherwood
1876		Graduates from Chestnut Ridge Primary School
1880		Graduates from Liberty Normal Institute
1881	9	Enters Liberty Normal Institute's "Teacher's Class"
	10	Obtains Second Grade Teacher's Certificate
1882	2.6	Transfers to Montgomery Union School, following her former professor Mr. Reuben Fraser, newly appointed Principal of the school
	4	Graduates from Montgomery Union School
	5.1	Starts teaching at Huntington District School
	9.6	Enters the Oswego State Normal School
1883		Graduates from the Oswego State Normal School; obtains a First Grade Teacher's Certificate; teaches at Bethel District School
1884		Teaches at Chestnut Ridge School, Sullivan County, New York
1886		Enters the Woman's Medical College of Pennsylvania
1889	3.14	Graduates from the Woman's Medical College of Pennsylvania Interns at the Nursery and Children's Hospital, Staten Island

Diary of Dr. Rosetta Hall 1892-1894

	11	Works as a physician for the New York Deaconess Home Begins medical missionary work in Hell's Kitchen in New York City; meets her future husband Rev. William James Hall, M.D. (b. January 16, 1860, Glen Buell, Ontario, Canada), who is in charge of the medical missionary work in the slums of New York
1890	8.21	Leaves Liberty, New York for Korea as a medical missionary, under the auspices of the Woman's Foreign Missionary Society of the Methodist Episcopal Church
	9.4	Boards the S.S. Oceanic in San Francisco
	9.24	Arrives in Yokohama
	10.10	Arrives in Pusan, Korea
	10.13	Arrives in Chemulpo, Korea
	10.14	Arrives in Seoul
	10.15	Starts medical work at Po Ku No Kwan, the firs Woman's Hospital and Dispensary established by the Methodist Episcopal Mission
	10.24	Selects two girls from the Ehwa-Haktang Mission School, O Waka San and Chom Tong Kim, for medical assistance training
1891	1.25	Chom-Tong is baptized as "Esther"
	1	Starts teaching physiology to five girls: Esther, O Waka San, Susanna, Pong Sun ("Mary Sparks Wheeler"), and Annie
	8.21	Travels to Chefoo, China, with Miss Bengel
	12.15	William James Hall arrives in Korea (Pusan) as a medical missionary for the Methodist Episcopal Church
1892	3	William goes on a country trip with George Heber Jones; Visits Pyongyang for the first time

Diary of Dr. Rosetta Hall 1892-1894

	6.27	Rosetta marries William James Hall
	7	Returns to Seoul from a honeymoon in Chefoo
	9	William is appointed to Pyongyang; Rosetta is appointed to Seoul
1893	3.15	Opens the East Gate Dispensary (Baldwin Dispensary) in Seoul
	5.24	Esther Kim marries Yousan Pak
	11.10	Rosetta and William's first son Sherwood is born in Seoul
1894	5.8	The Hall family arrives in Pyongyang with Esther and Yousan; begins medical work; begins instruction of the blind girl Pong-Nae O
	6.6	Evacuates to Seoul due to persecution
	8.1	Sino-Japanese War begins
	10.1	William leaves for Pyongyang
	11.19	William returns to Seoul, sick with typhus fever
	11.24	William dies
	12.10	Rosetta departs from Chemulpo to America with her son Sherwood and Esther and Yousan
	12.16	Arrives in Nagasaki
	12.18	Arrives in Kobe
	12.21	Boards the S.S. China in Yokohama for San Francisco
1895	1.6	Arrives in San Francisco
	1.14	Arrives in Liberty, New York

Diary of Dr. Rosetta Hall 1892-1894

	1.18	Gives birth to Edith Margaret in Liberty, New York
	2	Esther Pak enters the Liberty Union School; Yousan works at the Sherwood Farm
	4	Begins a biography of her late husband and fundraises for the establishment of the Hall Memorial Hospital in Pyongyang
	6.27	Rosetta's father Rosevelt R. Sherwood dies
	8	Rosetta visits her husband's family in Glen Buell, Ontario with her children and Esther and Yousan
	9	Esther Pak enters the Nursery and Children's Hospital of New York City; also studies for admission into the medical school
	10	Rosetta attends the Annual Meeting of the New York Branch of the Woman's Foreign Missionary Society (W.F.M.S.) in Brooklyn, October 16-18; visits Esther Pak at the hospital
1896	2	Visits New York and Middletown
	4	Attends a conference for the International Medical Missionary Society (I.M.S.S.), New York City
	5	Moves residence to 121 E. 45th Street with children and Yousan
	6	Moves into the New York Deaconess Home for work; sends children back to Liberty; Yousan takes a new job for the family of Rev. A.B. Sanford in New York
	6.22	Begins work at the New York Deaconess Home; works as the examining physician for the Christian Herald Fresh-Air Children Summer Camp at Mt. Lawn, Nyack until September
	9	Esther Pak enters the Baltimore Woman's Medical College

Diary of Dr. Rosetta Hall 1892-1894

	9.28	Rosetta works for the International Medical Missionary Society; moves back into 121 E. 45th Street residence with children
	10.28	Attends the General Executive meeting for the W.F.M.S. at Rochester, New York
1897	2.1	Establishment of the Hall Memorial Hospital in Pyongyang; Sherwood attends kindergarten until March
	5.20	Closes her work for I.M.M.S. at the Deaconess Home; decides to return to Korea
	5.22-30	Visits Esther Pak in Baltimore
	5.31	Arrives in Liberty, New York; finishes manuscripts of her husband's biography; Yousan also returns to Liberty to depart for Korea
	8	Publishes The Life of Rev. William James Hall, M.D. Yousan decides not to return to Korea and gets a new job at Mrs. Adgate's house, near the Sherwood farm
	9.6	Rosetta leaves Liberty for Korea with Sherwood and Edith Margaret; visits husband's family in Glen Buell, Ontario en-route to Korea
	10.11	Boards the S.S. Empress of India in Vancouver
	11.10	Arrives in Chemulpo
		Makes the first embossed book for the blind of Korea, pricked on oiled Korean mulberry paper by hand
1898	4.29	Leaves Seoul to start work in Pyongyang
	5.1	Arrives in Pyongyang
	5.23	Edith Margaret dies of dysentery
	6.18	Opens the Women's Dispensary of Extended Grace in Pyongyang, as well as the Mother-Baby Clinic and the School for the Blind

Diary of Dr. Rosetta Hall 1892-1894

1899	5	Attends the Annual Meeting in Seoul; embarks on a building project of the Edith Margaret Children's Wards
1900	1	The School for the Blind is built
	4.28	Yousan Pak dies in Baltimore of tuberculosis
	5.5	Rosetta's mother Phoebe G. Sherwood dies
	5	Esther Pak receives M.D. degree
	10	Esther Pak arrives in Korea
1901	3	Due to overwork, Rosetta recuperates in Chemulpo and Seoul
	5	Attends Annual Meeting in Seoul
	6.7	Departs for America with Sherwood
	6.22	Boards the S.S. Nippon Maru in Yokohama
	7.7	Arrives in San Francisco
	7	Arrives in Castile, New York
	8	Enters the Castile Sanatorium and stays for 8 months
	10	Attends the New York Branch Annual Meeting
1902	4.5	Discharged from the Sanatorium; moves to Brother Charles' home
	8.14	Leaves Liberty for Korea (via Europe)
	8.25	Visits husband's family in Canada for one week
	9.2	Boards the S.S. St. Paul in New York
	9.10	Arrives in London
	10.16	Boards the S.S. Glen Logan from Swansea to Batúm

Diary of Dr. Rosetta Hall 1892-1894

1903	3.18	Arrives in Seoul, Korea
		Works at the Women's Hospital of Extended Grace in Pyongyang with Esther Pak
1906	11	The Women's Hospital of Extended Grace in Pyongyang is burnt down
1908	9	The new Women's Hospital of Extended Grace in Pyongyang is built
		Sherwood completes the eighth grade at Pyongyang Foreign School and enters the Chefoo Boarding School
1909		Rosetta opens the Pyongyang School for the Deaf
1910	4.13	Esther Pak dies of tuberculosis
	6	Rosetta attends the Edinburgh World Missionary Conference as a delegate from Korea, and then takes a furlough in America
1911	4	Sherwood enrolls at the Mount Hermon School in Massachusetts
		Rosetta completes her furlough and returns to Korea
1912	3	Starts a Medical Training Class in Pyongyang with Mary Cutler, M.D.
1914	8	Enrolls three female students as auditors at the Government Medical School in Seoul: Soo-Kyong Ahn, Hae-Ji Kim, and Young-Heung Kim

The First Annual Convention on the Education of the Blind
And Deaf of the Far East is held in Pyongyang, August 11-14

1915	Sherwood enters Mount Union College in Alliance, Ohio
1917	Rosetta moves to Seoul; works at the East Gate Woman's Hospital and Dispensary

Diary of Dr. Rosetta Hall 1892-1894

1918		Takes a furlough; works as a physician for the Board of Health in Philadelphia; Sherwood is engaged to Marian Bottomley
		The three female students at the Government School obtain medical licenses
1920	9	Rosetta starts a Woman's Medical Training Class in Seoul
		Marian Bottomley enters the Woman's Medical College of Pennsylvania
1921		Rosetta serves as the director of the East Gate Woman's Hospital and Dispensary
		Opens a Women's Hospital in Chemulpo
1922	6.21	Sherwood and Marian Bottomley are married in Ohio
1923		Sherwood graduates from the Medical College at the University of Toronto
1924	6	Marian Bottomley graduates from the Woman's Medical College of Pennsylvania
1925	8.15	Sherwood and his wife leave for Korea
1927	2.18	Rosetta's grandson William James Hall is born
1928	9.4	The Woman's Medical Training Class in Seoul becomes the Kyong-Sung Woman's Medical Institute
	10.28	Sherwood opens the Haiju School of Hygiene for the Tuberculosis
1932	10.8	Second grandson Joseph Keightley is born
	12.3	Sherwood prints the first Christmas Seal (1932-1933) in Korea
1933	9.23	The Haiju Sanatorium dedicates its chapel to Rosetta
	11	The Woman's Medical Institute graduates its first students

Diary of Dr. Rosetta Hall 1892-1894

	11.25	Retires from the mission field; returns to America to take care of Brother Frank Sherwood in Groversville, New York
1934	9.12	Granddaughter Phyllis Marian is born
1936		Opens a medical practice in Groversville, New York
1938		Returns to Liberty and opens a medical practice
1943		Retires from medicine; moves to the Bancroft-Taylor Rest Home in Ocean Grove, New Jersey
1951	4.5	Dies in Ocean Grove, New Jersey. Ashes are interred at Yanghwajin Foreign Missionary Cemetery in Seoul

Index

Aeogae, 67, 141
Allen, Dr. Horace N., 46
Amah, 152, 153, 163
American Legation, 214
Aogi. *See* Aeogae
Appenzeller, Mrs. Henry G., 23, 54
Appenzeller, Rev. Henry G., 16, 29, 31, 35, 36, 54, 63, 71, 75, 126, 140, 203, 227
Asleep in Jesus, 226
Avison, Dr. Oliver R., 212
Baldwin Dispensary, 106, 119
Bengel, Margaret, 14, 15, 21, 23, 24, 32, 33, 41, 46, 56, 63, 111, 141, 209
Between the Lights: Thoughts for the Quiet Hour, 100
Bisbee, Herman, 55, 124
Bishop, Mrs. Isabella Bird, 174
Bismuth, 212
Blaine, James G., 115
Bonar, Horaitus, 34
Bottome, Margaret, 41
Bradley, Mrs. Emily Sherwood (Aunt Emily), 22
Bradley, Samuel, 22
Bradley, Sherwood Burr, 22

Brainard, Mary Gardiner, 138
British Consul, 158, 179, 196, 207, 210, 215
British Legation, 46, 214
Brooks, Phillips, 115
Brown, Dr. and Mrs. O. E., 56
Browning, Elizabeth Barrett, 228
Bunker, Mrs. Annie Ellers, 56, 98
Bunker, Rev. Dalziel L., 46, 56
Busteed, Dr. John B., 65, 120, 125, 126, 135, 141, 211, 227
Captain Kim, 193, 195, 197, 200, 207
Captain Thompson, 50
Captain, Tessensohn, 209
Catgut ligature, 34
Chang, Quen Sik, 69
Chefoo, 47, 50, 51, 58, 62
Chemulpo, 26, 47, 48, 61, 73, 75, 77, 136, 141, 188, 205, 209, 210, 211, 218, 220
China Inland Mission (C.I.M), 59, 60
Chow, Mrs., 33
Chung Wha, 223
Consecration, 226

Corbett, Rev. and Mrs. Hunter, D.D., 59
Cowen, Mrs., 21
Cowper, William, 38
Crealinau, Mr., 224
Crosby, Fanny, 226
Cutler, Dr. Mary M., 109, 127, 131, 137, 141, 142, 144, 173
Dombquey, Mr., 77
Dove Party, 23
Dowkoutt, Dr. and Mrs. George D., 100
Drew Theological Seminary, 73, 214
Drummond, Henry, 51
Duffield, Grace H., 43
East Gate, 106, 119, 127, 133
East Gate Dispensary. *See* Baldwin Dispensary
Emerson, Ralph Waldo, 23, 72, 217
Emmagene, 63
Enmun, 169
Euiju. *See* We Chu
Foster, Rev. R. S., D.D. (Bishop Foster), 139
Frey, Lulu E., 141
Fusan, 73
Gale, Mrs. James Scarth, 33
Gale, Rev. James Scarth, 33
Gardner, Mr., 207, 208, 209
Gifford, Rev. and Mrs. Daniel Lyman, 56
Glimpses of Fifty Years, 72
God Moves in Mysterious Ways, 38
Goforth, Rev. and Mrs., 59
Gray, Tempie, 20, 22
Greathouse, Clarence R., 61, 77
Greathouse, Mrs. M. E., 56, 61, 77, 136, 143
Hall, Mrs. Rosetta Sherwood, M.D.
 annual meetings, 65, 139, 176
 appointment to Pyong Yang, 140
 at Po Ku Nyo Kwan, 16, 25, 32, 33, 34, 107, 119
 at Pukhan Mountain, 129, 131, 132, 134, 136
 Baldwin Dispensary, 106, 119, 133
 birth of son Sherwood, 143, 145
 birthday card to Dr. William James Hall, 14
 birthday, 27th, 63
 birthday, 28th, 137
 birthday, 29th, 217
 case of ascites, 107
 case of scirrhus of breast (breast cancer), 107, 133

Dove Party, 25
fifth wedding anniversary, 227
honeymoon, 48, 51, 52, 53, 56, 60
illness of Miss Lewis, 41
in Pyong Yang, 188, 190, 192, 193, 195, 197, 199, 200, 202, 203, 205, 207
letter from Annie Cassidy, 86
letter from Dr. Scranton, 36
letter from Miss Rothweiler, 54
letter from Mother-in-law, 66
letter from Susanna, 94
letter from the Appenzellers, 54
letters from Dr. William James Hall, 12, 18, 38, 44, 108, 162, 165, 169, 170, 171, 172, 223
letters from Esther Kim, 26, 31, 80, 84, 90, 98, 103, 105, 110, 111, 123
letters from Mother, 39, 115, 126, 136, 139, 148, 149, 150, 167, 217
marriage, 30, 40
meeting Mrs. Isabella Bird Bishop, 174
Po Ku Nyo Kwan, 141
pregnacy, 133, 137, 142
return to Seoul from Pyong Yang, 209
second wedding anniversary, 213
South Gate Dispensary, 127, 133
trip to Aeogae, 67
visit to sanatorium, Chefoo, 59
wedding, 42, 46
Hall, Rev. William James, M.D.
appointment to Pyong Yang, 65, 140
at Pukhan Mountain, 129, 130, 132, 134, 136
birth of son Sherwood, 143, 145, 146
birthday gift to Dr. Rosetta Sherwood Hall, 63
birthday invitation letter from Miss Bengel, 15
caring the July 23, 1894 wounded soldiers, 218
country trips, 15, 17, 19, 22, 31, 32, 35, 127, 138, 154
death, 226

275

honeymoon, 48, 51, 52, 53, 56, 60
  in Rev. Appenzeller's letter, 126
  in Seoul, 63, 117, 154, 172, 173
  letter from Dr. Leonard, 178
  letter from Miss Rothweiler, 14, 54
  letter from the Appenzellers, 54
  letter to Dr. Leonard, 183
  letters from Mrs. Rosevelt R. Sherwood, 39, 218
  letters to Dr. Rosetta Sherwood Hall, 12, 37, 44, 108, 162, 165, 169, 170, 171, 172, 226
  list of correspondences 1892, 13
  marriage, 30, 66
  meeting Mrs. Isabella Bird Bishop, 174
  memorial service, 226
  purchase of Pyong Yang mission property, 102, 109
  Pyong Yang mission work, 109, 118, 187, 189, 191, 192, 193, 195, 197, 198, 199, 200, 202, 203, 205, 207, 208
  second wedding anniversary, 213
  special quote, 64
  spiritual birthday, 78
  trips to Pyong Yang, 63, 70, 74, 82, 101, 107, 138, 151, 153, 160, 161, 165, 173, 188, 198, 202, 207, 220, 221, 223
  wedding, 46
Hall, Sherwood, 143, 146, 151, 153, 163, 167, 188, 190, 192, 205, 209, 212, 217
Han, Rev. Suk Jin, 19, 198, 202, 214
Harris, Mary W., 141, 211
Havergal, Frances R., 63, 130
Hayes, Rutherford B., 115
Heard, Miss, 77
Heron, Mrs. John. W.. *See* Gale, Mrs. James Scarth
Hillier, Walter C., 46
Hoang, Mrs. Mary, 107, 113
Holm, Saxe, 135
Hugo, Victor, 129
Hunan Province, 59
Huntley, Lydia, 220
I Gave My Life for Thee. See Thy Life for Me

Ioge. See Aogae
Ipecacuanha, 212
Jackson, Helen Hunt, 49, 135
Jenkens, Mrs., 33
Jenkins, Robert Rutter, 188
Jones, Mrs. Margaret Bengel. *See* Bengel, Margaret
Jones, Rev. George Heber, 12, 15, 31, 32, 35, 46, 76, 77, 84, 141, 209
Judson, Emily C., 216
July 23, 1894 Event of Japan taking Seoul, 218
Junkin, Mrs. William M., 113
Junkin, Rev. William M., 214
kang, 102
Keble, John, 166
Keen, Mrs. J. F., 139
Kejah, 205
Kilborn, Dr. Omar, 13, 130
Kim, Esther (Chom Tong), 26, 28, 31, 63, 79, 80, 81, 90, 99, 103, 104, 105, 106, 110, 111, 112, 113, 120, 121, 122, 123, 124, 127, 176, 193, 200, 201, 204, 209, 217
marriage, 121
Kim, Rev. Chang Sik, 154, 157, 168, 169, 170, 191, 192, 193, 198, 199, 200, 201, 205, 221
Knowles, Mrs. J. H., 23

kukyong, 174, 189, 190, 192, 193, 204
Larcom, Lucy, 15
Lee, Mrs. Graham, 217
Lee, Rev. Graham, 101, 102, 110, 118, 217, 220, 221, 225, 227
Leonard, Adna Bradway, D.D., LL.D., 139, 177, 183
Lewis, Ella A., 29, 32, 35, 36, 41, 42, 56, 63, 69, 107, 114, 137, 141, 144, 145, 146
Livingstone, David, 82
London Standard, 224
Longfellow, Henry Wadsworth, 18, 106
Lowell, James Russell, 18, 27, 45, 46, 49, 53
Luther, Martin, 62
Lyon, Mary, 173
MacDonald, George, 31, 128
Mallalieu, Willard Francis, 63, 65
mammitis, 32
mapoo, 122, 123, 155
marrow, 190
McGill, Dr. William B., 32, 35, 42, 60, 69, 125, 127, 141, 160
McGill, Mrs. William B., 60, 69, 128
McIntosh, Miss, 59
McKee, Mr. and Mrs., 56

McKenzie, Rev. and Mrs. Murdock, 51, 59
McKenzie, Rev. William J., 161, 200, 202, 205, 207
Methodist Episcopal Mission South
   building of Pyong Yang Mission, 157, 160, 161

Moffett, Rev. Samuel A., 110, 118, 161, 176, 191, 196, 200, 202, 203, 205, 207, 214, 217, 220, 224, 226
Moore, John Ely, 146
Moore, Mrs. Samuel F., 131, 141
Moore, Rev. Samuel F., 132, 214
Moore, Thomas, 213
Mortimer, Favell Lee, 129
My Jesus I love Thee, 227
My King, 63
My Prayer, 117, 121, 175
My Wandering Boy Tonight, 77
New York Deaconess Home, 56
New York World, 224
Ni, Mr., 191, 201
Nienstead, Col. F. J. H., 77
No, Mr., 195
No, Sylvia (Amah), 176, 197, 200, 201, 205, 209, 211

Noble, Mrs. Mattie Wilcox, 63, 73, 74, 76, 87, 99, 100, 101, 106, 113, 125, 126, 135, 211, 218
Noble, Rev. William Arthur, 63, 73, 74, 75, 76, 110, 118, 125, 135, 141, 144, 211, 218, 219, 226
O, Suk Hyung, 191, 192, 193, 198, 201
Ohlinger, Rev. Franklin, 46, 141, 160, 168
Ohlinger, Willa, 101
Oswego, NY, 116
Pai Chai College, 141
Paine, Josephine O., 29, 63, 67, 87, 141
Pak, Mrs. Esther Kim. *See* Esther Kim (Chom Tong)
Pak, Yousan, 120, 122, 123, 124, 168, 189, 195, 196, 201, 209, 217, 219
Payne, Dr., 20
Pepsin, 212
Platt, Miss, 56
Pong Epie, 29
Pong Sunie (Mary Sparks Wheeler), 56, 58
Po-pe, 113, 114
Posan, 208
Presbyterian Mission North, 33, 59, 110
   purchase of Pyong Yang mission property, 118

Presbyterian Mission South, 214
Procter, Adelaide Anne, 148
Pukhan Mountain, 129, 135, 141, 154, 157, 214, 215
Pyeng-yang. *See* Pyong Yang
Pyoktanin, 212
Pyong An, 32, 81, 111
Pyong Yang, 17, 19, 63, 65, 77, 99, 102, 105, 107, 110, 111, 115, 118, 119, 127, 128, 138, 140, 141, 142, 150, 151, 154, 159, 161, 165, 168, 170, 173, 176, 177, 183, 184, 187, 190, 191, 192, 197, 199, 203, 204, 207, 208, 214, 215, 217, 219, 220, 221, 223, 225
Pyong Yang Theological Seminary, 19
Rachel, 113
Randall, Dr., 59
Reynolds, Mrs. William D., 131
Reynolds, Rev. William D., 214
Rothweiler, Louisa C., 13, 14, 17, 23, 24, 29, 39, 54, 141
S.S. Baltimore, 209
S.S. Chong Piong, 209
S.S. Genkai Maru, 47, 48, 50, 56, 61, 62
S.S. Satsuma Maru, 60

Sanderson, Miss, 60
Schiller, Freidrich, 128
scirrhus, 107, 133
Scott, Rev. S. H., 20, 22, 135
Scranton, Dr. William B., 36, 46, 128, 135, 140, 141, 154, 155, 156, 157, 158, 159, 160, 161, 165, 171, 173, 174, 175, 176, 177, 179, 183, 184, 185, 192, 194, 199, 202, 203, 206, 207, 208, 220, 226
Scranton, Max, 163
Scranton, Mrs. Mary Fitch (Dr. Scranton's mother), 23, 29, 46, 80, 120, 141, 174, 190
Scranton, Mrs. William B., 46, 56
Sea View Hotel, 51
Seoul, 19, 26, 31, 54, 61, 65, 67, 69, 73, 86, 94, 110, 119, 129, 131, 132, 135, 137, 141, 161, 165, 174, 178, 179, 183, 184, 188, 191, 192, 194, 199, 203, 206, 207, 210, 220, 223, 226
Shanghai, 13, 60
Sherwood, Annie, 19, 115
Sherwood, Dr. Rosetta. *See* Hall, Mrs. Rosetta Sherwooed, M.D.

Sherwood, Mrs. Emma C. Tice, 20
Sherwood, Mrs. Margaret Ver Noy, 47, 167
Sherwood, Mrs. Rosevelt R. (Mother), 19, 22, 39, 40, 115, 126, 127, 136, 139, 148, 150, 167, 217
Sherwood, Rev. Frank R., 126, 166, 168
Sherwood, Rosevelt R. (Father), 115, 136, 144, 167
shinju, 17
Si Pyung Won, 65
Siam, 66
Sill, John, 196, 202, 203, 210, 214
Sino-Japanese War, 218, 224
Skerrett, Joseph Salathiel, 209
Skidmore, Mrs. H. B., 20, 21, 100
Smith, Mrs. (sister-in-law of Thomas Lane), 218
Söul. *See* Seoul
South Gate, 127, 156
South Gate Dispensary, 127
Spts. Chloroform, 200
Steward's Hotel, 48, 50
Stoeckel, Dr. Louise M., 74
Stook, Mr. and Mrs., 59
Sugar Loaf Peak, 132

Susan, 113
Susanna, 93, 95, 113
Swallen, Mrs. Sallie Willison, 131, 141
Swallen, Mrs. William L.. *See* Swallen, Mrs. Sallie Willison
Swallen, Rev. William L., 110, 118
Sweeping through the Gates, 227
Sylvia. *See* No, Sylvia (Amah)
Ta Tong River, 77
Take My Life and Let it Be, 130
Tate, Martha Samuel, 215
Tate, Mattie Ingold, 214
The Changeling, 53
The Christian Advocate, 139, 177
The Mother-in-law, 40
The Ninety and Nine, 77
The Oriental Hotel, Kobe, 54
The Peep of Day, 129, 136
The Song of Hiawatha, 106
The Two Friends, 166
Thy Life for Me, 130
Thy Will be Done, 197
To My Husband, 216
Tong Hak, 119, 199, 208
Tong Shin, 59
Toy, Dr., 66
Tr. Opii Camph, 212
typhus fever, 141

Union Church, Seoul, 144
Villiers, Fredrick, 224
Vinton, Dr. C. C., 56, 136, 226
Vinton, Mrs. C. C., 36, 56, 60, 136
We Chu, 31, 81, 107, 110, 118, 160, 224, *See* Euiju
Webb, Mrs., 217
Wee Ju. *See* We Chu
Wesley, John, 32
Whang Hae Do, 118
Whang Ju, 223
White Lake, 115
Wilkes Barre, 74
Wilkinson, Mr., 159
Willard, Frances E., 63, 72, 122, 124
Wilson, Joe (Josiah), 22, 115, 116, 167, 217
Woman's Foreign Missionary Society (W.F.M.S.), 14, 28, 76, 139
Won San, 33, 141, 160
yangban, 33, 101
Yellow Sea, 50, 132
Yi, Mrs. Priscilla, 111, 113
You, Mr., 118, 120, 190

www.ingramcontent.com/pod-product-compliance
Lightning Source LLC
LaVergne TN
LVHW051545070426
835507LV00021B/2408